THE HERALD DIARY

No Moos is Good Moos

THE HERALD DIARY

DIARY

No Moos is Good Moos

Ken Smith

BLACK & WHITE PUBLISHING

First published 2018
by Black & White Publishing Ltd
Nautical House, 104 Commercial Street
Edinburgh, EH6 6NF

1 3 5 7 9 10 8 6 4 2   18 19 20 21

ISBN: 978 1 78530 179 7

The publisher has made every reasonable effort to contact copyright holders
of images in this book. Any errors are inadvertent and anyone who for any
reason has not been contacted is invited to write to the publisher so that a
full acknowledgement can be made in subsequent editions of this work.

A CIP catalogue record for this book is available from the British Library.

Typeset by Iolaire Typesetting, Newtonmore
Printed and bound by CPI Group (UK) Ltd, Croydon, CR0 4YY

Contents

Introduction

DESPITE the best efforts of some of those in power at home and abroad, it seems that every day something funny happens on the streets and in the homes of Scotland. And, fortunately for us, readers of *The Herald* – Glasgow's favourite newspaper – are famous for taking the time to jot down these tales and send them into the paper's daily Diary column.

They might be stories about the gems that the younger generation are forever coming out with, the gaffes of politicians, the shenanigans of Scottish football, the tribulations of trying to grow old gracefully or the wise-cracking ripostes of rocky relationships. One thing is for sure, whatever the topic, if something makes you smile then it will end up in The Diary.

And here we have gathered together the best of readers' stories from 2018 so that – hopefully! – we can help the smiles continue.

1

Let's Hear Your Banter

Ah the banter!
  Some of the more memorable lines heard are not skil-fully crafted jokes but simply remarks made in the spur of the moment which our readers are happy to pass on, as they are worth preserving.

STRESSFUL time, funerals. A reader tells us of a recent Glasgow funeral where a young relative of the deceased stopped the priest before the coffin was being taken into the chapel and said he wanted to place a picture of his late aunty's pet dog on the casket. The priest gently squeezed the chap's arm and told him: "It's a coffin, son – no' a sideboard."

A PARTICK reader swears to us he saw a young lad running along Dumbarton Road wearing a cape, so he jocularly shouted after him: "Are you a superhero?" and the chap shouted back: "Naw, I've no' paid fur ma haircut."

OLD insults that should be preserved. Now you don't hear the word dookin' much these days – getting kids to immerse their heads in a basin of water to capture an apple before they drown seems to be waning. But as Ed Hunter reminds us: "With regards to a chap with a florid complexion – 'Ah think he's been dookin' fur chips.'"

INSULTS that should be saved, continued. Now you hardly ever see anyone playing billiards these days as it is all pool or snooker. So it has probably been a while since anyone said to a loudmouth, as reader John Leonard recalled: "You could put three billiard balls in that mooth o' yours and still not get a cannon."

THE firm that ran the Christmas market in Glasgow's George Square has lost the contract, *The Herald* reported. Some folk thought it was a bit brash, it has to be said. As an old colleague memorably described it last Christmas: "The beer bar looked as enticing as the waiting lounge at Glasgow Airport on Fair Friday just before the last flight to Magaluf."

ARCHIE Knox, who was assistant manager with Alex Ferguson at Manchester United and Walter Smith at

Rangers, told the audience at a Waterstones author event at The Avenue in Newton Mearns that the first game after his arrival at Ibrox was Rangers losing to Motherwell.

Recalled Archie: "They were rebuilding the main stand at Ibrox at the time and when I walked in on the Monday morning one of the workmen on the stand shouted down, 'Hey Knox! You've made a big difference, haven't you?'"

HOW'S this for an argument? Deril Wyles in Stirling revealed: "Guy from the TV licence chapped my uncle's pal's door who told him he didnae have a telly, and the guy was like, 'You've got an aerial on your roof.'

"He replied: 'I've got a pint of milk in the fridge – disnae mean I've got a coo oot the back,' and shut the door."

AND so the hot weather continues, although some folk find it uncomfortable. *Still Game* actor Gavin Mitchell passed on the following conversation he had the other day: "Taxi driver: 'How was yer night?' Me: 'Awright. Yersel?' Taxi driver: 'Aye awright, just sittin' sweatin' ma a*** aff oan this PVC seat wi' this windae open thinking, *Whit am a dain' wi' ma life? Why did a no' try harder?*'"

OUR sister paper the *Evening Times* ran a story about a prisoner who absconded from jail being found in Cumbernauld. Steven McAvoy muses: "What's the point in escaping the jail if yir just going to go to Cumbernauld?"

GREAT weather at the weekend, with Glasgow's parks mobbed. A reader lounging in Kelvingrove Park heard a mother call her daughter over and firmly tell her to put on sunscreen. The daughter dubiously picked up the tube, read the label and asked: "Factor 50? What's in it when you squeeze it out? A blanket?" And for sheer daftness, Geraint Griffith says: "I hope my neighbours have a barbecue soon or I'm going to look rather stupid with all this salmon on my washing line."

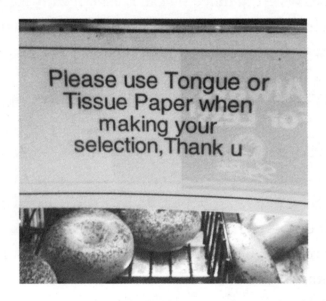

A READER swears to us he heard a wee lad in a park ask his dad: "Can I get an ice cream?"

"If you're good," said the dad.

"Good at what?" asked the boy.

"Buying your own ice cream," he was told.

A READER hears a woman in a Glasgow coffee shop explain to her pals: "The young girl in the hairdresser's was talking about her wedding and saying rather rudely that she didn't want any fat bridesmaids. It took all my effort not to lean over and say, 'Why? Do you not want any competition?'"

MODERN life explained by Liz Hackett, who says: "Life is a constant balancing act between wondering why you weren't invited to something and wondering how to get out of it."

TODAY'S daftness comes from Pete Firman, who says: "I spent the last three days alone trying to learn escapology. I need to get out more."

HONESTLY, it's just a joke, and we have nothing against such a fine place, but Martin Morrison gets in touch to muse: "There are only a handful of words in the English language that contain the letter sequence 'rrh'.

"I've listed a few. Gonorrhoea, diarrhoea, pyorrhoea and haemorrhoid. Oh, and Barrhead."

A GLASGOW reader heard a philosopher in his local pub declare: "Nothing ruins your Friday like suddenly realising it's Thursday."

DAFT gag of the day comes from a Lenzie reader who says: "My girlfriend says that sex is better when you are on your holidays.

"Well, that's a postcard I wasn't expecting."

WE don't often make political points in The Diary but we pass on the observation by Karl Sharro, who says: "Under communism, you buy everything from a single state outlet, whereas under fully mature capitalism you buy everything from Amazon."

DAFT gag of the day comes from a Milngavie reader who emails: "Went into a shop and said I wanted to buy stockings for the wife. 'Sheer?' the assistant asked. 'No, she's at home,' I replied. 'Does it matter?'"

TODAY'S piece of daftness comes from a Baillieston reader, who emails: "Our local Co-op was broken into last night and two dozen cases of Red Bull were stolen. I don't know how these people sleep at night."

GOOD to see the introduction of minimum alcohol pricing in Scotland this week, despite daft claims it will lead to booze trips across to England to stock up on gut-rot cider.

A reader in Glasgow's city centre yesterday heard a young woman coming out of a newsagent's shop and asking her pal: "Has minimum pricing also kicked in on chocolate? I mean, 75p for a Wispa!"

2

Glasgow

We cover the whole of Scotland in The Diary, but some stories are just pure Glasgow.

AMUSED to read in a TravelSupermarket survey that Glasgow's robust Partick area is rated as one of Britain's hip places to hang out – overtaking nearby Finnieston. Bumped into actor Jimmy Martin recently who was recalling the barber's shop at Partick Cross decades ago. The owner once told him about a customer coming in with his young son, who waited while "dad" got a haircut. Said Jimmy: "When he was finished he said to the barber, 'Would you cut the boy's hair while I nip into the bookies?' The barber cut away, but there was no sign of the father coming back and the barber said to the boy, 'He's taking his time.' The young lad replied he didn't know who he was and he had just asked him outside if he fancied a haircut."

A YOUNG woman revealed on a Facebook page for citizens of Glasgow's Dennistoun that: "This morning I went to fetch my washing off the line and all my underwear was gone. Feeling a little creeped out." Fellow Dennistonians expressed their disgust at such a theft, although one chap did reply: "My neighbour once came to my door asking if I'd stolen her underwear from the washing line. I nearly wet her pants!"

STILL great weather, although folk are saying they are losing their appetite in the heat. Tom Rafferty passes on the dilemma of the chap on a sweltering 38 bus in Glasgow the other day who answered his phone and declared: "Sweat's runnin' aff me ... Naw, no' really hungry ... Too hot ... Where you goin'? ... Get us a pie supper, hen ... Ten minutes, doll."

OUR introspective taxi-driver story reminded Derek Miller in Torrance: "Years ago, having attended a black-tie dinner at Glasgow's Crowne Plaza, I emerged, fully refreshed, and into the waiting cab. The driver was a jovial big fellow and we started chatting about football. 'Whut team dae ye support, big man?' he asked, and on noticing the bloke's 'Aye Ready' tattoo, I replied truthfully, 'Rangers, mate.'

"'Dae ye like the tunes, big man?' he asked. As soon as I nodded in the affirmative, he reached down the side of his seat, produced a flute, and belted out 'The Sash My Father Wore' with one hand, whilst driving with the other."

THE fire at the School of Art is incredibly sad, but thank you to Glasgow crime novelist Denise Mina for cheering us up with a story about the nearby ABC venue on Sauchiehall Street which was also engulfed that night. Denise said: "My pal fell down the ABC stairs when she wasn't wearing knickers. Her skirt rode up and she was so embarrassed that she pretended to be unconscious. A crowd gathered. Someone called 999. The ambulance crew must have been very angry. Where will chaotic, knickerless drunks go now?"

IT is Blood Donor Week, as donation centres remind folk they still need donations even though a lot of regular donors are away on holiday. It reminds us of a worker at the Glasgow donation centre who told us of a donor who concluded his session by saying: "Well, that's me, I'll not be back here again." Concerned staff asked if they had done something to offend but he replied: "No – it's just that when I had an operation, I was given nine pints of blood and now I've given you the nine pints back."

AVRIL Paton, painter of those great Glasgow tenement paintings, has her latest work, a cracking picture of Kelvingrove Art Gallery, put on display in the gallery. One of Avril's lesser known works is *Rita's Find*, which is of Glasgow's Paddy's Market. She once told us that when she was down there making her initial sketches, angry stallholders came up and demanded to know if she was spying on them "frae the social".

Quite why they thought government officials would use a sketch artist rather that someone with a camera for spotting benefit fraud was never explained.

WHERE did the time go? It's the 30th anniversary of the opening of the Glasgow Garden Festival, and we recall a reader who told us that a pal who busked with a violin outside bingo halls was called in to the dole office in those Thatcherite days and quizzed about his job-seeking. He had put himself down on the books as a violinist, believing no job would be found for him and he could carry on his indolent days on the broo. Said our reader: "I didn't see him for some months before visiting the Garden Festival. On entering the catering hall, I was amazed to see our man for the first time ever in a suit and black tie, sitting in the front row of the band and sawing his fiddle in a completely scunnered manner, having to cope with six months of gainful employment."

MAIRI Clark passes an office in Maryhill which has a sign outside stating that studio workshops are available to let. The sign states there is "24-hour axes". She assumes it is a misspelling of "access", but being Maryhill...

A GLASGOW reader was in his local when a chap told his pals: "What you read about me in the *Evening Times* today is true." After a shocked silence, he said: "I'm selling my couch."

COMEDIAN and broadcaster Hardeep Singh Kohli is of course the brother of Sanjeev Kohli, *Still Game*'s shopkeeper Navid. Hardeep was in Glasgow appearing at St Luke's in the Glasgow Comedy Festival, and he tells us: "Coming back to Glasgow, you realise how much you've missed the chat. As I'm cycling doon the road a young ne'er-do-well shouts out at me, 'Awright, Navid!'

"Not one to take my brother's credit, I huff 'I'm not Navid' between puffs, as I try to defy gravity up Great George Street. Quick as a flash he has a comeback: 'Aye, I know yer no' Navid, but it disnae half p*ss you off.'"

For an additional $5.00 we will provide you a receipt that will match what you told your spouse you paid!

A GLASGOW reader heard some young chaps in his local pub discussing the pros and cons of vegetarianism, when one of them declared: "Imagine being a vegan, stumbling home after a night out, and saying to yourself, 'I could fair go a cabbage supper.'"

PLANS have been announced to have a statue to South African leader Nelson Mandela erected in Glasgow, the first place in Britain to give him the Freedom of the City. We still recall when Nelson arrived in Glasgow for the ceremony – the late lamented Crocket's Ironmongers in West Nile Street had a sign in its window stating: "Mr Mandela – get your spare keys to the city cut here."

IT was Royal Ascot over the last few days – yes, didn't the Queen look lovely – and Scott McCarthy tells us: "I'm sorry that the fine chestnut colt Yabass faded at the finish of the Queen's Vase at Royal Ascot. I'd love to imagine punters in bookies' shops all over Glasgow shouting at the screens, 'Come on, Yabass!' Congratulations to the owners, though, for sneaking the name under the British Horseracing Authority's radar."

AH, we've all been there. Ian Craig in Strathaven gives us his view on Ryanair slashing its flights from Glasgow Airport: "Just wondered if I'm the only person in the west of Scotland delighted with the news.

"This will save my wife trawling through their website and trying to get me to fly to Timbuktu or some other equally obscure place that I don't really want to go to. Then having to join a queue well before departure at some God-awful hour before being dazzled by the garish yellow interior of the plane. Just hope that Edinburgh is next."

GOING to the cinema has taken a new turn, with Odeon refurbishing its cinemas at the Quay and East Kilbride to give film fans fully reclinable leather seats – you can easily have forty winks if the film doesn't hold your attention. Anyway, it allows Diary chum John Sword to reminisce: "My dad years ago told me about a friend who married an usherette from the Rio at Bearsden. At the church she walked down the aisle backwards.

"Younger readers won't get it."

3

Loving It

There are many twists and turns in the course of true love. Our readers share a few of these precious moments.

A READER heard some young lads in the pub at the weekend discussing how suspicious their girlfriends were. One lad topped the stories by declaring: "I took the girlfriend for a romantic weekend in Paris and when we got there I pointed over and said, 'There's the Eiffel Tower.' She just threw me a dirty look and snapped, 'I thought you said you'd never been to Paris before?'"

EVER taken revenge on a former boyfriend or girlfriend? A reader in Dublin says a girl on a bus was telling her friend that every week she still plays the same Lotto numbers as her ex. She explained that if he ever won he would have to cope with the news that the millions were divided in half and he had to share it with his former girlfriend.

PROVING that friends are all heart, a Glasgow reader heard a chap in his local declare that he had talked his pal out of leaving his wife. When the topers around him congratulated him on being so sensitive, he added: "I had to. Otherwise he'd expect me to help him move his stuff out – and he's three floors up."

A DENNISTOUN reader couldn't help smiling when she heard a chap in her local tell his girlfriend: "Do you know, in the six months we've been going out, we've not agreed on one thing."

"Seven," she replied.

A GLASGOW reader swears to us that a young lad in his local bar was telling his pals: "I got a text from the girlfriend saying 'Love you babe xxx', and after I replied 'Love you too' she said it would mean a lot to her if I started putting Xs at the end of my texts.

"So I ended my next text with 'Olivia, Heather, Sophie and Kirsty' and somehow all hell broke loose."

A WEST END woman tells us: "I had a woman's voice on my car's GPS giving me instructions on how to get to places, but then I discovered I could change it to a man's voice. I switched it over to the man, but all it ever said was, 'It's around here somewhere. Just keep driving.'"

A READER at his Ayrshire golf club tells us a fellow member confessed he was not really paying attention when his wife returned from a shopping trip to Glasgow and announced that she had bought a new dress. He glanced up from watching the Masters on the telly and said, "I like the zip down the front. Very sexy." His wife shouted back, 'That's the garment bag it's in, you idiot."

A BEARSDEN reader tells us about married life: "I woke up the other day and told my wife that I'd had a vivid dream in which she was arguing vehemently with me. So she then told me I had probably done something stupid to provoke the argument. And I found myself apologising to my wife for an argument which didn't actually take place."

A WEST END reader heard a young woman triumphantly tell her pals that she was celebrating the three-month anniversary of her new relationship. "Big deal," replied a pal. "I've had dishes in the sink longer than that."

TODAY'S daftness comes from a reader who emails: "My girlfriend said she slept with five men before she met me. I was only 20 minutes late."

A PIECE of whimsy from a female reader who emails: "Was in the hospital car park with my pal and I said to her, 'I thought we were here to get your X-ray back?' She replied, 'Yes, we are,' as she slashed a tyre with a Stanley knife. 'This is his car.'"

TRICKY thing, that Facebook. It now puts up pictures of events that happened years ago. A Bearsden reader says: "I shouldn't have commented on an old picture of my wife, 'You looked a lot better then.' I know that now."

STILL great, but very warm weather. Says Neil: "My wife likes it if I blow on her on days like this – but I'm not a fan."

FANTASTIC weather, but the heat can make folk a bit fractious. A reader in the Buchanan Galleries in Glasgow yesterday heard a couple snapping at each other while they walked in front of him until the woman eventually said: "I'm too tired to argue. Carry on without me."

TRICKY things, relationships. A Glasgow reader overheard a young beau in his local tell his pals: "Can't believe it. The girlfriend's not talking to me – says I ruined her birthday. But I didn't know it was her birthday so how could I have ruined it?"

A GLASGOW reader tells us she bumped into an old friend who was single and asked her if she was seeing someone. Her pal replied: "Put it this way, my mobile phone has its own side of the bed."

A READER in the West End overhears a woman telling her pal over coffee: "Came home the other day and my husband had cleared out the garage without me asking him to do it. Now I've got to try and work out what he's feeling guilty about."

AN AYRSHIRE reader tells us a fellow member in his golf club was telling him the other day: "I opened a kitchen cupboard and managed to catch a glass before it fell out on my head. I just put it back in the same spot to see if my wife's reflexes are as good as mine."

DENTURES. Barrie Crawford tells us: "An old friend of the family couldn't find her dentures. After searching up and down, she finally discovered her husband's dentures still in their box and that he was wearing hers. When she chastised him, his only comment was, 'I wondered why I'd been talking so much!'"

AN AYRSHIRE reader tells us wives' birthdays were being discussed in his golf club where one of the members declared: "I forgot my wife's birthday and told her, 'You can't expect me to remember your birthday when you never look any older.'"

"Did that work?" a fellow member asked him.

"Not in the least," he admitted.

THERE are times you have to agree with author Corinne Sullivan, who remarked the other day: "Couple sitting next to each other on the subway, and the woman is talking the man's ear off about her room-mate when the man goes, 'Katie, if you don't mind, I'm going to go into my head for a bit.' I now have my response to every conversation I want out of forevermore."

A GLASGOW reader getting the train into town swears he heard a woman bumping into an old pal tell her: "I recently ended a three-year relationship." She then added: "It's OK though, it wasn't mine."

A READER from Bearsden emails: "I was telling my son how technology was making his life a lot easier than mine when I was his age, and when he asked for an example I told him that he will never experience the anxiety of calling a girl's phone number and having to ask her dad if she's home."

THE TRIALS of married life as an Ayrshire reader emails us: "My wife just said, 'You weren't even listening, were you?' and I thought to myself, 'What a strange way to start a conversation.'"

A GLASGOW reader swears to us that he heard a young chap in his local announce: "My girlfriend's threatening to leave me because she claims I'm more interested in playing poker than in her. I think she's bluffing."

WE bump into an old colleague who swears to us that the letters editor on his newspaper received an epistle from a reader who stated: "My wife was about to file for a divorce when she read an article in your paper about how giving people a second chance was important in making a marriage work. So she changed her mind about the divorce. Anyway, long story short, could you please cancel my online subscription."

AN AYRSHIRE reader passes on a comment from a club member in the bar after a round of golf: "I noticed that the wife had put on her sexy underwear before I came over here, so that can only mean one thing...

"She's behind with the washing."

AH, it will soon be the time for dodgy chat-up lines at office Christmas parties. A reader shook his head last year when he heard a young chap tell a female after work in the pub: "You look great without glasses."

"I don't wear glasses," she told him, which gave him the opening to put on a pair of glasses and say: "Yes, but I do."

WE mentioned the chat-up lines in pubs as office Christmas parties approach, and a reader in Edinburgh says he heard the classic line last year uttered by a woman: "Do you come here often?"

The chap she was talking to smiled and said: "All the time."

"That's great," she replied. "In that case, do you know if the barman is seeing anybody?"

MARRIED life, continued. A chap in a Glasgow golf club tells his mates: "Every Saturday night I watch *Strictly Come Dancing* with the wife. She turned to me on Saturday and asked me who I wanted to win. Although I've watched it every week I couldn't name a single person who was on it."

A GLASGOW reader swears to us that a fellow toper in his local was being asked how his date with someone he met online had gone: "You know she said she had an infectious smile?" he told his pals. "Turned out it was cold sores."

A READER says he heard a young chap in the pub at the weekend announce: "I made my girlfriend's dreams come true by marrying her in a castle, although you wouldn't have thought it from the look on her face as we were bouncing around."

YOU can imagine the woe of Josh Billingsley who declares: "My pregnant wife texted me a selfie in a new dress and asked, 'Does it make my bum look big?' I texted back, 'Noo!' My phone autocorrected my response to 'Moo!'

"Please send help!"

4

A Class Apart

Children – they are either driving you demented or you love them to bits.

Here's what they've been up to.

WE do like the combination of innocence and deviousness that children sometimes portray. Reader Karen Beckett in Fairlie was recalling a neighbour's five-year-old who was visiting her who suddenly asked: "Can I have an ice pole?" Karen told her it was polite to wait to be asked. Seconds later the child piped up: "Is there something you want to ask me?"

A WEST END reader hears a woman gulping Pinot Grigio at the next table to him in an Ashton Lane bar tell her pals: "Every evening my neighbour's daughter practises piano with what sounds like her face."

A WALK through the St Enoch Centre in Glasgow shows a few empty shops as the centre awaits the demolition of the old BHS store at one end and the building of a new cinema and restaurant complex. We still remember a previous stroll through the centre when we passed a mum asking her youngster in the buggy she was pushing for a drink from the carton of juice he was holding, but he wouldn't hand it over.

She told him: "I wipe your a***. The least you can do is share your drink."

SOMEHOW it was National Biscuit Day yesterday, and a reader recalled: "Do you remember the thrill when you went home as a lad and found a biscuit tin on the kitchen table, and you eagerly opened it up hoping to wolf down a Bourbon or a Custard Cream only to discover your ma's sewing kit?"

A GLASGOW teacher tells us she was talking to her primary class about colours and had asked them what their favourite colour was.

One wee girl said "turquoise" which was a bit different from the others, so the teacher turned to the board and said: "That's a very good one. How do you spell it?"

The girl immediately said: "I meant to say red."

THE NEWS that the Scottish Government has banned wild animals in travelling circuses reminds us of the teacher who was explaining to her colleagues that she had been to a circus where an elephant was made to wear a skirt while performing.

"It was a right shame," said the teacher. "The poor thing was peeing all the time."

"Was it incontinent?" asked an anxious colleague.

"No, it was in Stranraer," came the reply.

OLD gag alert as Iain Martin tells us: "With all the news about the rare red moon I am reminded of the teacher explaining about the solar system and asking the class, 'Where is Mars?'

"Little Johnnie raises his hand and says, 'Please, Miss, you're sitting on it.'"

STILL enjoying the kids being off school? A Southside reader on the train into town heard these wise words from a woman telling her travelling companion: "Friend on Facebook posted that she was brimming with joy that all her kids were home from school and university just now. You see, it's lies like that which are putting me off social media."

TALKING of teachers, a Southside reader sends us the gag: "I remember my teacher telling me that looking out of the window wouldn't get me anywhere.

"Did I have a smug look on my face later on in life when I handed him his burger and fries at the drive-through."

WE asked for the best excuses for being late, and Jim McInally tells us: "A few years ago I was teaching at Broughton

High School. One morning a student came in late. She had a note from her mother explaining that she was late because mother and daughter had been trapped in the bathroom for an hour by a spider."

EXCUSES for being late, continued. A St Andrews reader tells us his dad told him of two brothers who went home from school for their lunch. One of them arrived back late and, when asked why by the teacher, said: "Please, sir, I got the wee spoon the day."

THE *Herald* reported that tickets for Disneyland in America have gone up considerably, with tickets for peak days rising to nearly £100. It reminds us of the teacher who got a phone call from an angry mother who said her son had arrived home from gym without his towel, stating that someone must have taken it and adding: "No one respects other people's property these days." Hoping it would turn up, the teacher asked for a description and she said: "Striped, with Disneyland Hotel written on it."

OUR trip down memory lane just now is school jotters, and Neil in Ayr recalls: "Talk of whether they were covered in brown paper or wallpaper reminds me of when I was in first year at Kilmarnock Academy and had to cover all my textbooks. I was given some rather floral wallpaper to use, so quickly decided to use it inside out to avoid ridicule in class.

However, after a particularly wet walk home found all my books had stuck together and could not be separated. I then realised I had been given pre-pasted wallpaper.

Amendment to chip pan fire story

In the *Advertiser* of September 19, we reported on p3 that a chip pan fire broke out on September 14, at Friar Grove, Buxton. We have been asked to point out that it was in fact a "smouldering pan of noodles."

WE should close the book on our old school-jotter stories, but before we do, Barham Brummage in Bathgate tells us: "During my teaching career I had many different types of covering: wallpaper, brown paper, greaseproof paper, but the one that stands out literally was when I had been nagging a lad to get his jotter covered for several days.

"Eventually he turned up beaming from ear to lug with a covering of . . . carpet.

"A good chunk of thick pile had been glued to the front and back. I suppose he would be the only kid who had to Hoover his jotter."

MORE on school jotters, as former teacher Jean Miller memorably tells us: "When I had a Primary Three class they wrote a daily news page to encourage their handwriting, grammar, spelling and sentence extension. Didn't know what to do when a child wrote, 'I had to get up early today and help my mum push her boyfriend's van to start before my dad came back.'

"Sought advice from the Infant Mistress, as they were called in the eighties. She said, 'Tear it out and say to the child that you are sorry that you spilt your coffee on it at break time.' So I did."

TODAY'S piece of educational daftness comes from a Hillhead reader who emails: "There's no point using Latin phrases if you don't understand what they mean, and vice versa."

THE *Herald* news story about the Glasgow teacher who was drunk at school brings to mind, of course, the classic yarn of the teacher being given a box at Christmas with a present in it. The box was leaking so the teacher drew her finger along the bottom, licked it and asked, "White wine?" Replied the youngster, "No, Miss, a puppy."

WE read that it is Anti-Bullying Week. A reader in Partick tells us: "The guy who bullied me in secondary school is still taking my lunch money.

"But to be fair to him, he does give me a pretty big pizza slice in Greggs."

SILLY gag time, as Bob Swanston says: "I bought my great nephew an Action Man for his birthday, but he told me that he really wanted a Red Indian.

"Since then I've been trying to put a brave face on it."

A YOUNG person explains to us how life has changed: "When I was very young, the most terrifying part of going into the sea when on holiday was thinking that a shark might attack you. Now my biggest fear is leaving my phone on the beach."

OUR trip down memory lane this week was old school jotters, and a reader reminds us of the teacher who gathered in her class's jotters and discovered one lad had scrawled the sectarian slogan "UVF 1690" on it. He then diminished the impact somewhat by adding "Remember the Boing".

TODAY'S peace of daftness comes from a Lenzie reader who says: "Took the family up to Aberfoyle at the weekend. Son staring out the window at the fields suddenly announces, 'Didn't realise so many sheep were into paintballing.'"

A LENZIE reader muses: "I passed a restaurant the other day that had a sign saying 'Kids Eat Free' and I thought to myself, 'Kids always eat free.'

"I mean, when I take my brood to the restaurant never once has one of them put his hand on the bill and said, 'Don't worry, Dad, I'll get this.'"

AN EXCITABLE news report in *The Herald* claimed that families travelling to the beach at Troon were "terrorised by hundreds of drunken youths". A Glasgow reader tells us: "Many years ago I witnessed absolutely disgusting behaviour on Troon beach. I saw a man and woman having an almighty argument in front of loads of kids.

"Suddenly the woman smacked the chap on the head and it all kicked off. There was a massive brawl and someone called the police. This poor officer turned up on his own and took out his baton to the man. Then the chap snatched the baton and hit the police officer. Then, out of nowhere, a crocodile crept up and stole all the sausages."

A POLLOKSHIELDS mother confesses: "My three-year-old asked if he could have for his breakfast the Maltesers his grandma gave him the previous day when she called round.

"I emphatically told him he could not, saying it would be bad for his teeth and inappropriate for breakfast.

"My argument was probably strengthened by the fact I had

eaten them the night before when he was in bed and I was watching my favourite hospital drama on the telly."

WE really must end our false-teeth stories, but a reader reminds us of The Diary story some time ago of the grandmother who told us she didn't notice her granddaughter coming into the bathroom just as she was taking her set of false teeth out. Her hopes that it would go unnoticed were dashed when the little one went racing downstairs shouting at her brother: "Come and see Gran. She's doing tricks."

WE are going far down memory lane, as a reader continues our best excuses for being late with the recollection: "I taught in the Gorbals many years ago and one little boy's excuse for being late in the days of boxed-in beds in tenements was, 'I couldnae sclim ower ma granny.'"

PARENTING skills, continued. Says a Cambuslang reader: "My granddaughter was looking through some family photograph albums and asked me why so many people in those days had red eyes.

"I was about to explain to her about using camera flashes close up but decided, what the heck, and told her instead about the demon uprisings in the seventies.

"Seemed to impress her."

REARING children, continued. A reader tells us: "I remember taking my nephew to the soft play for the first time.

Worried about letting him climb on his own, I stood at the bottom shouting instructions, and at a point where there was a low ceiling, I shouted, 'Duck, Archie, duck,' to which he turned to me and replied, 'Quack quack,' just as his head bumped into it."

BUMPED into our old chum journalist Paul Drury, who tells us: "Kind shopper at Glasgow supermarket notices till operator explaining to a girl of about nine that she does not have enough for her sweets. Chivalrous shopper offers to pay the difference but was taken aback when he was asked for £2.50. Nevertheless, he brandishes a tenner and says, 'Take it off this.'

"The wee girl skips away and the guy says jokingly, 'Bet she tries that every week.'

"The till operator's face fell. 'You mean she's not with you? I just gave her your change!'"

SO are your children a bit obsessive about their mobile phones, always wondering who is contacting them? A Bishopbriggs reader tells us: "Was sitting in the lounge with my son watching the football on the telly when his phone, which was in the kitchen, pinged to say he had a message. He immediately got up and went through to the kitchen to read the message, which said, 'Just make a cup of tea while you're there. Dad.'"

A WHITECRAIGS reader fears that his teenage daughter might be an evil genius. After warning her that he was going to confiscate her mobile phone at night because she was contacting her friends late into the small hours, he carried out his threat, took her phone and left it in his bedroom. Hours later he was abruptly woken as she had set the alarm for four in the morning before he'd snatched it from her.

THE stress of being a teenager. A reader heard his daughter look up from her mobile phone and state: "Some people have written 'Happy Birthday' on my timeline without any exclamation marks. It's as if they don't even care."

A NEWTON MEARNS reader swears to us that his teenage daughter announced: "My friends say that I'm self-absorbed, so I took a long, hard look at myself. Beautiful."

BRINGING up grandchildren, continued. A reader confesses she was reading an article in *The Herald* about an online course on Jacobites in which, said *The Herald*: "Participants will study the Jacobite campaigns from the flight to France of James II in 1688." She was spluttering at the newspaper calling him James II instead of his Scottish title, James VII, and her grandson asked what was wrong. When she read the sentence out to him he merely asked: "When were aeroplanes invented?"

GRANNIES are the best, aren't they? Sandra Williams in North Berwick tells us: "Overheard in North Berwick High Street. Grandmother asks young grandson what his bright green lollipop tastes of. 'Lime,' he replies. 'That's good for you,' she says."

CHILDREN'S tales, continued. Says Margaret Forbes in Kilmacolm: "Your story about the child frightened of the draught reminded me of the time my mother and sister came home drookit after heavy rain. My mother said, 'We were caught in that rain!' And so I said fearfully, 'What does the rain do to you when it catches you?'"

Talking of mothers, an East Kilbride reader asks: "I wonder how many tragedies my mother actually prevented when me and my siblings went out to play and she stood at the door shouting at us, 'Be careful!'"

WE mentioned getting youngsters to behave at the airport while flying out for the Easter break, and Margaret Thomson tells us: "When my granddaughter was four, we went as a family group to Florida. At Glasgow Airport, we went through all the queues, check-in, passport control, body scan, etc., which took over an hour. When we finally emerged in the departure lounge, my granddaughter asked, 'Are we in Florida now?'"

A RATHER tetchy reader phones to tell us: "It's Father's Day this month. My message to teenagers is get something that will really make your dad happy on Father's Day. A flat."

5
Student Days

As new student flats pop up around our main cities, we bring you some of the stories of our bright young hopes for the future.

AS the new intake of students prepares to head off to university, a former Glasgow Uni student tells us of a group years ago getting together for a drink, when one of them who had disappeared for a while told his pals: "You'll never guess what I wrote on the toilet wall."

One of his pals was sober enough to tell him: "We left the Union half an hour ago, ya eejit. We're back in my flat."

OUR recent tales of student life remind a former Glasgow Uni student of a neighbour knocking at the door at two in the morning and announcing that he couldn't sleep. Our reader's flatmate, who answered the door, drunkenly told him: "Well, you're in luck. Our party's still going so come on in."

WE asked about student flats, and a Glasgow reader tells us that, years ago, he and his chums played the classic trick on a flatmate who was annoying them. They balanced a bucket of water over his partly open bedroom door. "Of course he spotted it," says our reader.

"Rather smugly he slowly removed it and took it to the kitchen sink to empty it. He then failed to notice that we'd removed the waste pipe below the sink.

"Happy days."

A READER on the train from Mount Florida to Central Station yesterday heard a young girl look up from her mobile phone and tell her pal: "Did you see that Selena Gomez got a kidney from her best pal?" After a pause, she added: "And you wouldnae even lend me yer student ID card."

CONGRATULATIONS on Glasgow Uni going through on *University Challenge* after a close victory over Emmanuel College, Cambridge. We liked the comment of Dr Belinda Brooks-Gordon after seeing the programme, who remarked: "Speaking as an academic, it's just a delight to see eight students without their phones for half an hour."

And Dani Cugini on the Emmanuel team said afterwards: "I love presenter Jeremy Paxman. He gets so indignant if people don't recognise the poet William Blake, but he reads out the science cards like they're in Klingon."

TODAY'S daft observation of the day comes from a West End reader, who emails: "A big thank you to the Student Loans Company for getting me through university. I don't think I can ever repay you."

OUR colourful tales of infestations remind Willie Young of post-student days living in a West End flat with pals above a bakery and having an influx of cockroaches.

Says Willie: "One of my flatmates worked at United Biscuits, where the pest-control man suggested we put down bicarbonate of soda and sugar on baking foil. Successful? Fantastic.

"The only snag was we had to have the kitchen redecorated as the cockroaches exploded. What a sight when we turned on the light in the morning."

SOMEHOW we slithered into tales of flat infestations, and Stuart Miller in Linlithgow recalls: "In a West End flat in the seventies we lived above a kebab restaurant, which sent cockroaches up the pipes. When the Rentokil man came he asked me to capture a few at night so he could assess the problem. A few weeks later my brother-in-law came across my matchbox with a cockroach, so jokingly put it in his wife's coffee. As it eventually floated to the surface, she screamed in horror, but he laughingly assured her it was just a plastic fake. 'Er not exactly,' I told him. Cue more screaming."

WE pass on the comment from American college professor Marian Viorica, who is not impressed by the ability of her students to get up in the morning. As she put it: "I once taught an 8 am college class. So many grandparents died that semester. I then moved my class to 3 pm. No more deaths. And that, my friends, is how I save lives."

OUR tales of student life remind Sandy Tuckerman: "I had a flatmate who would Hoover his bedsheets once a term, whether they needed it or not."

AS our flat infestation stories continue to run around, reader David Steel tells us: "Reminds me of sharing a communal flat on Pollokshaws Road with one friend embellishing his life with a pet hamster, which ran about the living room inside its ball.

"However, one day the hamster went missing, and after much searching we reckoned it had escaped to city life.

"Three months later we were leaving, and the owner sent in cleaners to make it ready for the next tenants.

"We arrived to reclaim our deposit, and the owner produced a dead hamster which had been found in the toilet brush holder. To add insult to injury he took £30 off our deposit because we weren't meant to have pets."

MANY parents will have sympathy for broadcaster Anneka Rice, who said: "Messaged my son, 'Dear Son, I transferred £80 to you in a sunny weekendy moment of love, except you'll have realised by now my thumb juddered and I sent £800. This is not what I meant to do. Obviously. Please get in touch.' No reply so far."

6

No Business like Show Business

Scots love to meet the famous – and if the famous can tell a story against themselves, then so much the better.

GOOD to see Scottish women being explained to Americans. Paisley-born film star Gerard Butler was on a late-night chat show in the States when he explained: "You can't get away with much in Scotland." He said he was in a bar back in Scotland when a woman who had been staring over at him came over and said: "You know, I know your face from the telly – but I'm not gonna tell you that, because it's going to give you a big ******* head!" Host Seth Meyers asked: "Is that Scottish flirting?"

INTERESTING musing from comedian Kate Robbins, who appeared at Glasgow's King's Theatre not so long ago in the show *Fifty Shades of Beige*. Said Kate: "A few years ago I met Princess Anne at a charity event. In the pre-show line-up she asked me what I did. I said, 'I'm an impressionist,' to which she replied, 'Do you have an exhibition on anywhere?'"

ALL this sobering commemoration of the 20th anniversary of the death of Diana, Princess of Wales reminds Tim Malseed of a story involving a friend of his. The friend's gran phoned very early in the morning, telling him urgently: "Quick, put your television on. Something has happened to Diana in Paris – she's been chased into a tunnel by Pavarotti on a scooter."

GOOD to see Glasgow-born songwriter Bill Martin of "Congratulations" fame going on stage at the Edinburgh Fringe to talk about his career. Gordon Wright tells us that Bill confided that he had met Stones' singer Mick Jagger recently and commented on the number of wrinkles on his face. "They're laughter lines," replied Mick.

"Nothing's that funny," said Bill.

GLASGOW'S Susan Calman was all dolled up yesterday for a red-carpet appearance by this year's *Strictly Come Dancing* contestants. As she later commented on her chances of winning, the diminutive comedian said: "To do well on *Strictly* I may need to be more 'tabloid'. [Coughs] In 1991 I was late returning *Puppet Master* to Azad Video. I paid the fine."

OUR tales of bands remind Billy Sinclair: "When Glasgow was European City of Culture in 1990, I was in the reception of the media centre in St Enoch Square when Deacon Blue came in for a press call. No matter who you were, you couldn't get past reception without signing in.

"The receptionist asked for their name and Ricky Ross told her, 'Deacon Blue,' which she wrote down. But as the band went past her she called them back, saying, 'I've got Deacon's name,' pointing at Ricky, 'but I need aw youse names before you can go through.'"

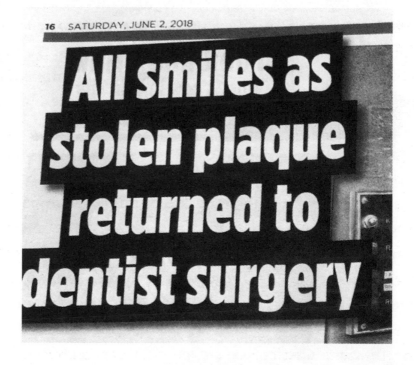

16 SATURDAY, JUNE 2, 2018

All smiles as stolen plaque returned to dentist surgery

GLASGOW-BORN author Ryan O'Neill, now living in Australia, has been shortlisted for the Australian book award, the Miles Franklin Award, for his irreverent book taking the mickey out of Aussie culture, *Their Brilliant Careers*. It seems the old phrase about "you can take the boy out of Glasgow" is true, as Ryan tells us: "I've been in Australia about 13 years, but as Australians never tire of telling me, I still have my Glaswegian accent.

"In a shop the assistant asked me, 'Anything else?' and I said, 'No thanks, that's all.' After we walked out, my friend who was with me said in a shocked voice, 'Why did you call him an asshole?'"

THE news that the BBC is to pay £850,000 in costs to Sir Cliff Richard after he sued them in a privacy case reminds us of the yarn our late lamented editor Arnold Kemp told of the *Scotsman*'s extremely erudite drama critic Charles Graves once being sent to review a Cliff concert in Edinburgh. The disgruntled Graves devoted most of the review to the jugglers who were the warm-up act, making many scholarly references to the history of their art. He mentioned Cliff only in the final paragraph, which was chopped off in the composing room to make the review fit the space, leaving confused readers the next day wondering why Cliff Richard never actually featured in a review of his show.

AS TV comedy series *Dad's Army* celebrates its 50th anniversary, surviving cast member Ian Lavender, who played Private Pike, ruefully revealed in the *Radio Times* that when he did a one-man show he would bring out the scarf that Pike frequently wore on the series and explained: "The scarf got a round of applause. I have to work an hour just to get a round of applause, but I just bring the scarf out and it gets one straightaway."

CULTURES collide, it seems, as folk head to Edinburgh for the Festival. The Rev. Richard Coles, one-time *Strictly* dancer, giving talks at the Fringe, explained yesterday: "Tremendous entertainment on the train to Edinburgh as someone who isn't, but could be, Gwyneth Paltrow, requires to know the provenance and vegan credentials of the tea being briskly served by the Geordie LNER ladies."

And self-styled bubbleologist Louis Pearl, who has impressed audiences for years at the Fringe with his gravity-defying bubble tricks, tells us he recently had a lad about nine up on stage who volunteered to be put in a bubble. Having a chat with him, Louis saw the boy's arm was in a cast and asked what had happened. "A dog bit it," said the youngster. Trying for a laugh, Louis then asked: "What happened to the dog?" Instead of smiling, the boy said with a straight face: "He got castrated."

FORMER singer-turned-minister Richard Coles was indeed a popular figure on the last season of *Strictly Come Dancing*, although his style was more wooden than the pews in his church. He was recounting at the weekend that he went to visit his mother in hospital and a nurse on the ward said: "Mrs Coles, is this your famous son, the *Strictly* vicar?" His mother merely replied: "Yes, but he was awful, so no need to fuss."

JOHN Cleese is in America publicising his rather underwhelming TV series, *Hold the Sunset*. We liked his reply when he was asked by our sister paper *USA Today* where his humour came from. Cleese replied: "It comes from a little man in Cardiff. He's just wonderfully funny. I read the postcards and do pretty much what he tells me. He told me recently they're not his ideas. He gets his ideas from a lady in Swindon who refuses to say where she gets her ideas."

THE *Radio Times* is asking folk to vote for their favourite television crime drama, with STV's *Taggart* in the shortlist. We remember a reader watching an episode of *Taggart* in France. It still had the original spoken English but with French subtitles. Our reader noticed that when Taggart, the late, great Mark McManus, unwrapped a fish supper, scowled and shouted: "Where's ma pickled onion?" the translator admitted defeat and merely put him saying on the screen: "*Bon appétit.*"

DEALING with hecklers. New York stand-up Mark Normand says he was interrupted the other night by an audience member who shouted: "You're white, what do you know about racism?" Mark's sharp response was: "Are you kidding? We invented it."

LOTS of folk enjoyed the royal wedding, although there were a few eyebrows raised at Prince Harry being made the Earl of Dumbarton. As Stephen McGowan commented: "Being made the Earl of Dumbarton as a wedding present? I'd take the toaster." And council cutbacks in local services led to Alan McGinley stating: "I live in West Dunbartonshire and the fact that Harry is now Earl of Dumbarton has unleashed a fury of expectation among the locals that the bloomin' grass might actually get cut."

MEETING someone famous, continued. Amongst the original line-up of the Rolling Stones was Scottish blues pianist Ian Stewart. Reader David Corstorphine tells us: "In the early sixties my granny and her sister, my great-aunt Phemie, worked at one of the knitwear factories in Cellardyke. One day, four young men or, as Phemie recalled, 'long-haired Nellies', arrived at the front desk, where Phemie was stationed. The men wanted in to speak to the lassies, but Phemie refused them entry. 'Do you know who we are?' asked the blond one.
    "Phemie told him, 'Ah'm no' carin' whoa ye are, yer no' gettin in tae spaik tae the lassies an' disturb their work!' At that point, management arrived and apologised to the Rolling Stones, who were in the village to meet founding member Ian Stewart's aunt Helen and had agreed to visit the factory.

I don't think Phemie ever appreciated how famous these long-haired Nellies would become, nor that she spoke so forcibly to Charlie Watts, Keith Richards, Ian Stewart and the late Brian Jones."

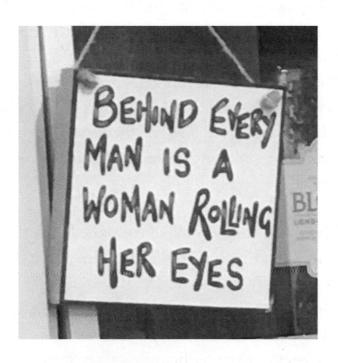

GOOD to see the Chic Murray play at Òran Mór this week, *A Funny Place for a Window*, getting a five-star review by *Herald* critic Mary Brennan. Chic is played by Dave Anderson, who actually lived a few doors away from Chic in the West End. Dave once told me he was standing outside his house one night when Chic walked past, obviously heading to the pub for a quick one before they closed.

Chic, though, caught Dave's eye and told him: "Just out

walking the dog." The thing was, Chic didn't have a dog. But to enhance his tale, every few yards he would stop and whistle on his imaginary mutt to catch up with him.

OUR story yesterday, about when the great Scots comedian Chic Murray lived in Glasgow's West End and couldn't stop making jokes when he bumped into people, reminded a reader of actor Finlay Welsh once saying that he bumped into Chic on Byres Road and they stopped for a chat.

At the end Chic asked: "Oh, by the way, Finlay, when we met just now, was I coming down Byres Road or was I going up?"

"Well, as I'm on my way up to the BBC to do a voiceover, you must have been coming down," replied Finlay.

"Oh, that's good," said Chic, "I'll have had my lunch then."

IT can happen to the best, it seems. Harry Potter writer JK Rowling told her fans on social media yesterday: "The great thing about editing is how you get to look back on the triumphant moment after your 19th readthough when you you were sure yuo'd caugth all the the typoes, and hat yourself for beng such a stupid, smug barstard."

AND while folk were not bothered about the royal baby, the idea of folk camping outside the hospital where the baby was born surprised one or two people. As the social-media site of Irish bookmakers Paddy Power put it: "Some folk have been waiting outside a hospital for 15 days for a baby they have no connection with. I can't be bothered waiting three minutes for my microwave meal to cook properly. Two minutes will do; lukewarm is fine."

OUR toilet tales cannot pass without at least one mention of these complicated train toilets.

As broadcaster Gyles Brandreth once related after a visit to Yorkshire: "I was outside the WC, pressed the button, the door opened and a poor sod inside turned frantically towards me, unable to staunch his flow. As he waved his arms in alarm, his spray went everywhere. 'Shut the door!' he cried as his trousers fell to his ankles. Then I pressed the button on the outside just as he pressed the button on the inside, so the closing door reopened – that's when he slipped."

OUR mention of the book being launched about sixties Glasgow group The Beatstalkers reminds a reader of when the band was booked to play at the Dennistoun Palais but couldn't appear as they had gone to a London recording studio to make a record. Instead, cardboard cut-outs of the band were put on the stage. After the support act The Bo-Weevils had performed, a phone on the stage rang and the Palais manager went over and answered it, and it was The Beatstalkers phoning from London. The crowd was screaming with delight.

Our old chum Eddie Tobin, then manager of The

Bo-Weevils, later said: "I presume they were paid an enormous fee for not appearing and we did all the work and got buttons."

NEVER knew so many readers had bumped into the legendary Chic Murray. Says musical Roy Gullane: "An erstwhile band member had met Chic and jokingly invited him to his stag night. The great man very graciously accepted the invitation. We spotted him waiting at the bar and our groom-to-be approached him with a hearty, 'Chic. Chic. We're over here.' The great man turned towards us and without batting an eye began to shout through the crowded bar, 'Where were you with the fast car? I was standing there like an idiot with the money!'"

CLYDEBANK stand-up Kevin Bridges has passed his driving test – 12 years after taking his first lesson. To be fair, his career got busy so he left driving for a bit. It reminds us of *The Herald* reader in America who told us: "When I moved to New Orleans in 1980, I drove to the test centre with my UK licence. Being August, it was 98 degrees Fahrenheit with 98 per cent humidity. The tester, being at least 25 stone, suggested I go out to my car, back it out of the parking space and drive it into the one next to it while she looked out the window of the air-conditioned office. And so I passed."

ACTRESS Julie Walters has been spotted at the Silverburn shopping centre filming for her role as the mother of a Scottish country and western star. We well remember when Julie spoke at a *Herald* book event and explained that she originally trained as a nurse before acting but never felt entirely comfortable in the job.

This was brought home to her on night duty on a coronary ward when a heart monitor emitted a piercing note. Before she could react, a medical student started pummelling the heart of the patient – a large Irish chap who sat up with a start and abruptly punched the medical student's lights out. It was then they discovered that the lead attached to him had accidentally come adrift.

TALKING of Alexa, a Glasgow reader swears he asked, while hosting a Boxing Day party that was going on too long: "Alexa, send everyone home." He claims the electronic device then played a Sydney Devine recording.

AMONG the movies out for Christmas is a remake of Agatha Christie's *Murder on the Orient Express*. John Henderson recalls an interview with Richard Goodwin, producer of the 1974 original, and many say better, version of the film in which he said the only problem he could recall dealing with so many stars in the one film was Vanessa Redgrave, then a member of the Workers Revolutionary Party, trying to convert the canteen workers and making political speeches at lunchtime. Eventually, he said, the canteen staff marched on management to demand that Vanessa was sent to talk to someone else.

OUR story about comedian Ken Dodd turning 90 reminds David Miller of Ken's gig at the Glasgow Pavilion this summer. Says David: "He told the audience how he woke up one morning with an attractive lady lying beside him. 'Have you been there all night?' he asked. 'Go back to sleep and finish your dream,' she replied."

RADIO 1 is 50 years old tomorrow. Scottish boxing legend Ken Buchanan recalled in his autobiography flying back to Edinburgh after retaining his world title in America. Hundreds of well-wishers in tartan were waiting to welcome home the hero.

The pilot announced passengers were to disembark quickly as there were important people on board who were to leave last. After the plane emptied Buchanan looked round and saw Radio 1 DJ Ed "Stewpot" Stewart still sitting there. Ed looked out the window and said: "My first visit to Edinburgh and look at the reception!" The pilot came back and explained who the actual VIP was.

A READER wonders if the statue of Nelson Mandela proposed for Glasgow will get the ultimate Glasgow accolade of a traffic cone on top of it. The strangest story we ever heard about the Duke of Wellington statue in Glasgow with the traffic cone was when Princess Diana's "love rat", to give him his tabloid sobriquet, James Hewitt was appearing in a BBC Scotland chat show with disgraced PR boss Max Clifford. Both men went for a drink afterwards and Hewitt suddenly clambered up the Wellington statue, knocked off the traffic cone and shouted down: "I won't see a national hero vilified." A strange cove indeed.

MEMORABLE audience reaction, continued. Says Sue Forsyth in Bearsden: "Gerard Kelly, the late, much-loved silly boy of panto, was the star of Iain Heggie's serious one-hander *King of Scotland* at the Citizens, where the language was coarse to say the least, but entirely in context. An elderly couple in front of us had obviously never seen Gerard out of panto mode, and they constantly tutted loudly until the lady eventually said out loud, 'Aw son – there's nae need fur that kinda language.'

"They appeared pleased when the Citizens staff asked them to leave."

BUMPED into playwright Peter McDougall at Òran Mór's annual Whisky Awards, where he tells me that he is writing a play about his hospital visits after a stroke, entitled *Vampire Clinic* – it's to do with all the blood samples they take – which is being staged as part of the venue's A Play, A Pie and A Pint series. Says Peter: "I remember talking to Willie McIlvanney once about his stroke and the side effects of taking Warfarin. Willie, being the great wordsmith that he was, described it as 'the physical manifestation of boils'. I'm no' the wordsmith Willie was as I just describe it as a rash."

Incidentally, Peter, looking very well, was not partaking of whisky at the awards night. As he put it: "I know people swear by whisky for a convivial discourse with friends, but I'm from Greenock – whisky tends to affect folk from there differently."

YES, congratulations to the royal couple of course. But as Simon Holland put it: "Wife shouts through, 'Kate had her baby!' I reply, 'That's cool. Tell her I said congrats.' And then I sit there thinking that I didn't know we knew anyone called Kate." Many people were happy with the news, others not so much. As a reader emails us: "Do you know, it's been quite nice to watch the news and be irritated by something other than Donald Trump or Brexit for a few hours. A change really is as good as a rest."

CHANCE meetings with famous folk, continued. Says David Knight: "Forty odd years ago my pal's dad, a member of the R&A, was entering the Clubhouse at St Andrews.

"He observed the uniformed club porter stiffly address a plus-fours-attired American and overheard the immortal sentence, 'Ah dinnae care if yer name's Bing Crosby, ye cannae come in the clubhoose!'

"Anxious to demonstrate Scottish hospitality, our man signed said crooner in and bought him a pint."

FULL marks to reader Jim Scott, though, who has managed to combine the royal wedding and our recent stories about comedian Chic Murray. Says Jim: "The news that Harry has been bestowed the title Earl of Dumbarton reminds me of the Chic Murray comment, 'A man said to me if you sit here you can see Dumbarton Rock. I sat there all day and it never moved an inch.'"

WE asked for your tales of meeting famous folk, and retired *Daily Record* journalist Jim Davis recalls that he was once sent to a charity golf event at Renfrew to interview volatile racing driver James Hunt. Says Jim: "The *Record* had got phone calls from readers complaining about Hunt wearing grubby jeans and a T-shirt, with one describing him as, 'lookin' as if he's jist fell oot a midden. The weans ur getting a right bad example set here, so they urr.'

"Hunt was in the bar beside an immaculate Sean Connery, Henry Cooper and Dickie Henderson. I got out, 'Mr Hunt, our *Daily Record* readers are complaining that your appearance is downright scruffy. And they say you're setting a bad example to the kids. What's your response?' His memorable reply in a cut-glass accent was, 'You can tell your readers that they are confusing me with someone who actually gives a ****.'"

SINGER Mica Paris is to star in a new production of the musical *Fame* at Glasgow's King's Theatre at the end of July. We remember when Mica had her first hit "My One Temptation" and was appearing at Glasgow's Tron Theatre. She later said: "I was 18 and just starting out. The Glasgow audiences were kind to me, though. One guy, a big, burly, macho Scotsman, came backstage at the end of that Tron show in tears, he'd been so moved by the music. Drying his eyes, he politely asked for an autograph, but made me promise not to mention to anyone that he'd been 'greetin' like a big wean'."

BBC reporter Tina Daheley went all sniffy about popular culture by declaring on social media: "A reminder that more people applied for the TV programme *Love Island* this year than Oxford/Cambridge University."

Someone promptly replied: "A reminder that it doesn't cost 28 grand to go on *Love Island*."

WE asked about telling folk what you do for a living, and writer and actor Stuart Hepburn tells us: "I was once approached by a rather well-oiled guest at a family wedding who enquired, 'So what do you do?' I answered, 'I am an actor,' and he said, 'Yes, but what do you do for a living?'"

TODAY'S piece of daftness comes from a reader who asks: "How many *Countdown* contestants does it take to change a BLIHBULGT?"

7

Will Do for Your Work

Most folk spend a third of their lives at work, so it is not unusual that many Diary stories come from there.

GLASGOW'S West End summed up beautifully as Rony Bridges, supporter of the Starchild charity for educating kids in Uganda, tells us: "What a week. Urgently needed a plumber and a tiler but all too busy so went to a play in the West End. Who is in the audience? Our tiler. Who's in the play? Our plumber!"

TALES of apprentices to mark Scottish Apprenticeship Week, and Raymond Lowe at Scottish Engineering tells us: "I was the apprentice instructor at Babcock's in Renfrew in the mid-seventies. At the lunch break I was approached by a number of the apprentices complaining that the water coming out of the urn was rather cloudy. On examination I found a boil-in-the-bag curry with rice in the urn. Ten out of ten for initiative. I wonder if he became the managing director?"

WE asked about telling folk what you do for a living and Peter Warren tells us: "In the sixties I worked as an apprentice plater in Fairfield's shipyard when I met my future wife at the Locarno. When we started dating she asked me what I worked at, and I told her I was a plater. Sometime later she asked me if there was any chance of getting her ma a half tea set.

"Coming up for 49 years married in August."

A READER who works in Glasgow's city centre phones to tell us: "Our office computers were down today and our manager came out and told us all that we had to do everything manually.

"It took me a while to find a pack of cards so that I could get on with my game of solitaire."

OUR tales of pies remind Louie Macari in Motherwell: "At the Glengarnock steelworks in the seventies, computers then filled up a room and data-input units were large metal cases which generated a fair amount of heat. An engineer called out to a fault opened the lid to discover a paper bag inside with a pie in it being kept warm. He held up the bag and was about to berate the operators when the owner of the pie turned up for his lunch. Not being a match for the heavily built steelworker, he just said to him, 'Your pie's ready,' and handed the bag over before proceeding to investigate the fault."

NO, it's not an old gag – we prefer the term classic. Anyway, we asked about telling folk what you do for a living, and Barry McGirr tells us: "Northern comedian Mick Miller told the tale he was stacking supermarket shelves with soap powder as a youth when a girl he'd dated passed him and hissed, 'You told me you were in the Red Arrows!'

"'No I didn't,' was his reply. 'I said I was in the aerial display team.'"

UNIVERSAL EXTRAS, which provides extras for television and film work, is having an audition in Glasgow due to the growing number of productions in Scotland. We remember a chum telling us he appeared in a scene in *Outlander* where he had to stand on a windswept hillside alongside other clansmen, a couple of whom were on horses. After standing there in the freezing cold he was delighted to see the director halting filming and dispatching a runner up the hill with blankets. Alas they were immediately put on the horses.

RECRUITMENT consultancy Robert Half says that almost two in five businesses take just two weeks to discover that they have hired the wrong person, with over a third of business bosses saying the reason is that people were found to be lying on their CVs. A recruiter once told us of an interview where the candidate was asked: "I see from your CV that your interests include politics. Who is the Prime Minister?" After a lengthy pause the graduate replied: "Oh, I said I was interested in politics, but I'm not obsessed by it."

TODAY'S the deadline for putting in your tax return if you are self-employed – no need to thank me for the reminder. As radio producer Ed Morrish, who left the BBC to work as a freelancer, put it: "I have just paid tax by myself for the first time. If you need me, therefore, I'll be in the *Question Time* audience, shouting about bringing back hanging."

ARTIST Ed Hunter tells us: "I remember very long ago when, as a spotty 17-year-old, I had a job with Glasgow

Corporation delivering wages to the nightshift workers at Govan cleansing. I was then picked up by a chauffeur in an Austin Princess to return to the City Chambers. As we pulled up at traffic lights at Edmiston Drive I was seated with my feet up on the wages box eating a banana. Outside the car the two guys looking in were Ralph Brand and Jimmy Millar of Rangers. They had a 'Who-the-hell-is-that?' look on their faces."

IT is Scottish Apprenticeship Week, which reminds us of when the dance performance Sparr, about the Gaels who transformed shipbuilding in Glasgow, was put on in Govan's Big Shed. Choreographer Norman Douglas revealed he had been a shipyard apprentice in the woodcutting section, and because he was the most nimble due to his then dancing hobby, he was instructed to "jump the wall" every Friday and bring back a bottle of whisky. The cash came from a whip-round, until one Friday, nervous about being caught, he dropped the bottle, which smashed, incurring the wrath of the woodcutting team. Next week he had to pay for the bottle out of his meagre apprentice wages, leaving him skint for the rest of the week.

WE mentioned conversations about what you do for a living, and Bob Byiers recalls: "A young chap, many years ago, who worked in the whisky industry, was on a night out at the dancin' when his partner of the moment asked him what he did. 'I work in a bond,' he replied. Clearly impressed, the young lady then asked, 'Oh, what instrument do you play?'"

TERRIBLE news about M&S planning to close 100 stores. As a former member of staff bitterly emails us: "Lovingly wrapped. In a creamy white envelope. With gorgeously detailed fine gold writing. And a first-class stamp. This isn't just any P45. This is an M&S P45."

OUR tales of being tardy at work remind Duncan Shaw in Kilwinning: "Back in the seventies when Glasgow Corporation had a bus works in Victoria Road I was walking across the yard on my way into work one morning in the company of an older workmate. It has to be said this was some time after when we should have clocked in. We were joined by the boss, whose only comment, as it turned out, was, 'Late!' Without so much as a sideways glance my friend's response was, 'So are we.' End of conversation."

WE have never had anything but excellent service from staff when we have visited, so we are conflicted when a reader emails The Diary: "My student son is playing the world's biggest game of hide and seek – he's got a job as a member of staff at B&Q."

OUR tales of excuses for being late remind Gerry MacKenzie: "When Strathclyde Police was formed, a young cop from

Oban transferred to Glasgow and acquired digs with a 'polis-approved' landlady. One bitter winter morning he was well late for work and told the gnarled old sergeant it was so cold in his tiny bedsit he left his electric blanket on. It used up all the coins in his electricity meter and rendered his electric alarm clock unpowered and useless. The sergeant stared directly at him for ages, shook his head and said, 'Aye, OK.'"

SO what's your best excuse for being late? There was a luvvie get-together at Sarti's Italian restaurant in Glasgow's Renfield Street for some Royal Conservatoire of Scotland former and current staff.

Alison Forsyth, former director of BAFTA Scotland, and the first director of the Scottish Drama Training Network, was unusually late. After 40 minutes Alison burst through the door with the memorable words: "A seagull s*** in my handbag."

ADA McDonald writes: "There may be an age limit to the stories you like to use in the Diary," and we reassure her that no, there is not. Anyway, it was our story about a secretary typing on a manual typewriter that reminded her of her aunt, a secretary with the Scottish Co-op Wholesale Society, who once told her of walking to work when she heard a window in the tenement she was passing being raised, and the agitated woman inside shouting down to her husband the unforgettable line: "Wullie! Wullie! Ye're away wi' the wrang teeth!"

A GLASGOW reader emails: "A colleague has retired after nearly 30 years with our company and the management were making a big thing about how she never took a day off sick. They called her dedicated.

"We always just called her the woman who kept on giving us all the flu."

OUR apprentice stories remind Alan Kerr in Tillicoultry: "When I was a student apprentice in Babcock & Wilcox, I was sitting in the work's canteen at lunchtime listening keenly to all the chat of the men at the table. With some few minutes remaining before the horn summoned us back to work, I stood up, leaving some food still on my plate. 'Where ur ye guan, son?' I was asked. 'No hungry?'

"I replied, 'It's not that. I need to go to the toilet before I go back.'

"'Sit doon and finish your dinner,' I was commanded. 'Just you remember – we eat and drink in oor time, but pee in theirs.'"

SCOTTISH Apprenticeship Week just now and Jim Allan in Cellardyke recalls: "I worked temporarily for MacDonald Aircraft near Kinross, where my apprentice wage just covered my digs, and I was horrified when the foreman told me on pay day, 'We a' pit hawf-a-croon a week intae a sweep an' whaever's clock number comes up wins the pot. So, see's yer money.' Very reluctantly I handed over my two-and-six, leaving me with less than £2 towards my rent. The clock number was drawn and, to my delight, it was mine. Over three weeks' wages in one fell swoop. Next Friday the foreman demanded my money again and amazingly I won again. The following week he told me there had been a decision that temporary apprentices were no longer eligible."

A GLASGOW reader swears to us that a young lad in his local was telling his pals about a recent job interview, and he told them: "The guy doing the interview looked at the form I'd filled in and said I was asking for quite a high salary considering I had no experience in their line of work. I explained that was because the work is much harder when you don't know what you're doing."

And we don't believe the reader who claimed: "I went for a job as an Argos delivery driver. Turned up three hours late for the interview and they said, 'Congratulations, you qualify for the job.'"

CROMAR'S in St Andrews has been named Scotland's best fish and chip shop for the second year running. We always liked owner Colin Cromar's explanation of how he got into the business. "I fancied a girl who worked in the Anstruther Fish Bar. I thought I would get a job there myself and ask her out. Twenty years later I was still working there."

OUR apprentice stories have suggested they are a gullible lot so we should end with a tale showing they were not that daft. Stuart Roberts in Switzerland remembers his apprenticeship at Rolls-Royce in Hillington when the apprentices "would use the lathe to turn out 10p-sized metal discs so we could get drinks out the machine".

A NEWSPAPER article about the 35th anniversary of the death of fighter ace Douglas Bader, who flew with artificial legs, reminds our old photographic chum John Young of when legendary Glasgow photographer Jack Middleton, who walked with a limp after childhood polio, was sent to photograph Bader at a memorial garden in Cupar. Says John: "Bader saw a limping Jack approaching and angrily said, 'Are you taking the mickey?' Jack merely replied, 'No, I thought you were.'"

TALKING about the great Cunard liners, entertainer Jimmie MacGregor rounds off our apprentice stories by recalling: "We were filming *The White Heather Club* on board the QE2 just before it was launched at Clydebank. As I was descending a gangplank I met a young apprentice coming up. 'Wherrs a' the burds?' he enquired, expecting to meet *The White Heather Club*'s dancers. I had to inform him that there wiz nae burds, as they had broken for lunch. He swore, then cheerfully added, 'And here's me went and combed up a' ma herr ana' tae.'"

AND our tale about the apprentice boiling the curry in the tea urn reminds a reader: "A colleague popped an egg into the kettle she was boiling for the office morning tea. One of the men discovered this and, grabbing a spoon, fished the egg out of the kettle and threw it into the bin, screaming at her, 'Do you realise where that has been?'"

A WORKER in a Glasgow office was impressed when his boss came up to a fellow worker and told her cheerily: 'You've been volunteered to . . .'" She interrupted her boss and said: "I think you'll find that the word is 'voluntold'."

APPRENTICES, continued. Says Marie Murray: "My late father was a maintenance engineer and the factory had a machine making machine parts, which was operated by a knee switch.

"My father told a poor unfortunate apprentice that the machine was voice operated, sat down, and said 'Go!' while pressing the knee switch. Of course, the machine part popped out on cue. The apprentice sat down, said 'Go', and, naturally, nothing happened. My father had lots of sport suggesting the fellow spoke louder, quieter, whisper, should even sing the command, all to no avail while a crowd watched."

WE asked about conversations where you tell folk what you do for a living, and Russell Smith in Kilbirnie says: "Bothered some years ago by an over-zealous waiter in an Indian restaurant. I responded to his latest of several questions of where did I work with 'HM Customs and Revenue Glasgow'. End of questions."

A HYNDLAND reader reports a dilemma that many of us face these days. She says: "I wake up saying to myself that I have so much to do and worry that there are not enough hours in the day. A couple of hours later I'm somehow doing a quiz on Facebook to discover what my gangster name would be."

TODAY'S piece of daftness comes from a reader who emails: "I was just thinking that the human brain is such an amazing thing – but then I realised who was telling me that – my brain."

8

Cheers

After spending so much time at work, it is not surprising that so many folk still nip into their local for a drink and a chat. Here are their pub and socialising stories.

SEEMINGLY there is a carbon dioxide shortage which could affect beer supplies. Pub chain Wetherspoons says it will review the situation in the next few days, however a "Spoons" customer phones The Diary to explain: "Regulars are advised that if they bring a straw there's a couple of weeks' worth in the carpets."

THE *Herald* news story that the grounds of Burns Cottage are to be planted with the crops of his era makes our mind wander to when Alex Ferguson owned the other Burns Cottage – a pub on Glasgow's Paisley Road West. No idea what it's called now. We just remember a woman telling us there was a band playing at the Cottage one night and they were all invited to someone's party in Govan afterwards. There was a sing-song and when the band's singer was asked to give them a number he loftily declared that he only sang for money. A penny was thrown at him with the instruction, "Now sing." He did.

THINKING of having a party at Christmas? A Glasgow reader tells us a work colleague alleges that when he held a Christmas party a few years ago in his West End flat he got so fed up with so many folk, half of whom he did not know, staying on into the small hours that he slipped outside and phoned the cops to complain about the noise, and just as he wished, a police car arrived shortly afterwards and told him to turn the music off because of complaints, and he managed to shuffle folk out.

A NEWTON MEARNS reader passes on: "My friend was telling me that bringing up three kids of preschool age meant she had to say no to many dinner-party invitations.

"When she eventually went out for dinner at friends, she automatically started cutting the chicken of the person sitting next to her."

WE savoured a few whisky stories last week, which reminded Andy Bryson in Ardrossan: "Around 1970 I worked as a 'shop boy' for Couper Wilkie's Wine Merchant in Saltcoats. A customer asked for our best whisky, and I indicated that the Glenlivet distilled in 1936 was probably the best and it was over £30. He said that would be perfect and I reached up to the top shelf to get the bottle. Couper saw me stretching up and ventured out of the office to oversee the transaction. I was just wrapping it when the customer asked for six bottles of ginger ale. Couper asked the customer if it was to be used with the Glenlivet and when the answer was 'yes' he took it from me, unwrapped it, put it back on the shelf and handed the customer a bottle of Bells, saying, 'You are not putting

1970 Canada Dry into 1936 malt whisky.' Customer went away quite happy, having saved about £25."

PUB chain Wetherspoons, which appears to have a pub on every street corner in Glasgow's city centre, has decided to stop using social media. Chairman Tim Martin told the BBC it will be good for society in general, stating if people "limited their social media to half an hour a day, they'd be mentally and physically better off". He added: "I find most people I know waste their time on it. A lot of them say they know they waste their time on it, but they struggle to get off it." A bemused reader emails: "So a bit like drinking in a Wetherspoons pub?"

WE have, we must admit, more than a fair share of pub stories in the Diary. Jimmy Nimmo in Ayr adds to the oeuvre by recalling: "A few years ago my wife and I found an ancient coaching house off the M6 for lunch and my wife excused herself to go to the Ladies. She was gone a few minutes when suddenly a bright light above the bar started flashing, and an alarm began loudly ringing. I was quite disturbed by this, but the locals seemed unmoved – at least till my wife came back, and she got a standing ovation.

"Turned out that in the Ladies' loo there was a doll of a red-faced Scotsman in a kilt, and a notice stating, 'If you want to know what the Scotsman has under his kilt – pull the string.' The string had two purposes – to lift the kilt and secondly to activate the flashing light and alarm."

THAT cheap and cheerful raucous bar Yates's Wine Lodge on Glasgow's Sauchiehall Street has closed – probably going to be student flats like every other gap site in the city – but anyway, we liked the former customers bemoaning its disappearance on social media, with one Glasgow chap telling his pal: "Mind breakdancing in here while you were on the sick with a bad back?"

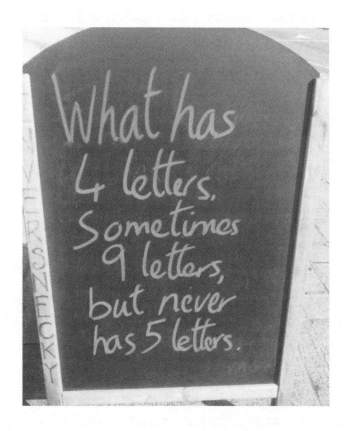

TRAVEL site TripAdvisor lists complaints, but we do like it when establishments reply. Someone was unhappy with Glasgow's great whisky bar The Pot Still and wrote that they were ignored at the bar. Pot Still management viewed the security tape and explained: "You came to the bar at 13:32:51, you turned away at 13:33:11 so all told you spent 20 seconds waiting before leaving. The youngest Scotch we sell waits three years in cask before it's even considered a whisky, let alone ready to be bottled. The oldest whisky we have waited 50 years before being bottled. When it went into cask, no one knew who Sergeant Pepper was and the UK was trying to get INTO Europe.

"If you feel 20 seconds is too long in your life to hang on in that company, then maybe you're not ready for whisky yet."

ONE of Glasgow's loveliest publicans, Elaine Scott, has retired from that great whisky and traditional music bar in Finnieston, the Ben Nevis. We like the interview in the trade magazine *Dram* where Elaine talks about the famous people who have called in, particularly as the Ben is so near the Hydro. Her list included Dolly Parton's drummer but then she added the memorable explanation: "He was just passing the time while he washed his drawers in the laundrette across the road."

THE popular Bag O' Nails pub in Dumbarton Road in Partick was named as Independent Bar of the Year in *Dram* magazine's Scottish Bar and Pub Awards.

Owner Mark Lappin, a music fan, tells me it was named after the first club in Britain that Jimi Hendrix played at, thus denying a Partick rumour I heard that it was named after the looks of the drinkers when the pub was previously the rather feisty Partick Tavern.

THE *Herald* reported that the Edinburgh Fringe will be the first festival to allow folk to use contactless technology on their credit and debit cards to tip street performers because of the reduction in people carrying cash. Not everyone though is happy with contactless payments. As a Liam Forrest revealed on social media yesterday: "Lost my bank card last night and some dafty's just used the contactless at Crown Stores. Do me a favour, mate – bring me a wee tin of Irn-Bru. I've got some hangover."

OUR false-teeth stories have perhaps inevitably led to a number of readers sending us the classic tale of the Glasgow chap at the formal dinner who had forgotten to put in his teeth, and the guest next to him saying: "I think I can help you. Give me a couple of minutes – my premises are just down the road." He reappeared a short time later and handed over a set of dentures which fitted perfectly.

"Great fit," said the man. "You must be an excellent dentist."

"I'm not a dentist," he said. "I'm an undertaker."

OUR tale of the cinema usherette who walked down the aisle at her wedding backwards has entertainer Andy Cameron reminiscing.

He said: "The Wee Royal, in Main Street Bri'gton, had forms rather than individual seats so the usherette would put you in at one end and tell the rest to 'shove alang a bit'.

"The result was that the one at the other end was dumped into the aisle and promptly ran back to the other end to start the process all over.

"It was a sort of Magic Roundabout before the telly."

OUR tales of old cinemas remind David Purdie: "On Saturday afternoons my brother and I used to go to the Grand in Stockbridge, which was a bit rough and ready. The toilet had an emergency exit that opened out on to the street by using a push bar. The rowdier elements would deputise one of their number to pay to get in, and he would then go to the toilet, open the door and half of Stockbridge would pour in for free.

"During a Tarzan film I was in the Gents just as an invasion was happening.

"The manager rushed in and chucked everybody out, including me who had legally paid. When the programme ended, my brother emerged totally unaware that I hadn't returned from the loo."

OUR stories about barbers reminds an Ayrshire reader of the tale of the minister who was getting shaved by the local barber, who had obviously been out on a bender the night before as his hand was shaking and he nicked the minister's chin a couple of times, drawing blood. "That's the whisky that causes that," said the minister disapprovingly.

"That's right," replied the barber. "It does make your skin awfy tender."

THE lights are about to come up on our old cinema stories, but time for Neil Dunn to tell us: "Many years ago I had an unpaid job as a monitor for the Saturday morning kids' matinee at the Waverley cinema in Shawlands. Free entry without queuing was the only payment and my only task, apart from spotting smokers, was to guard the emergency exit to stop anyone attempting to leave before 'The Queen' was finished playing. Can't think of this catching on nowadays."

AS the Burns Suppers wind down, Ian Lyell tells us: "At the Mauchline Burns Club, events organiser Malcolm Noble, before the meal, asked the company very solicitously if all those who were diabetic could raise their hand. Several did. Malcolm's response, 'Well, you won't need the tablet on your plate. Pass it to somebody else.'"

YOU'VE got to love Hue and Cry singer Pat Kane for his somewhat pretentious use of language. He took to social media this week to declare: "Wean 2 and I laughing and crying at *Paddington* last night. But weird ideologically. Immigration references obvious, but liberal middle class is near sanctified here and Daddy Brown clearly involved in financial innovation that unravels the very social pluralism they proclaim."

Understandably someone had to comment: "Mate, it's a film about a talking bear."

A READER coming out of Cineworld in Glasgow tells us of the chap in front of him who had just left a screening and told the girl with him that he had found some of the film hard to believe. When she asked him what he meant he replied: "Well, that bit where he's in a hotel room and immediately knows how the shower works."

A READER in Arizona of all places sends us a link to a joke page in her local newspaper which tells us about our national drink: "I went to the liquor store Friday afternoon on my bicycle, bought a bottle of Scotch and put it in the bicycle basket. As I was about to leave, I thought to myself that if I fell off the bicycle, the bottle would break. So I drank all the Scotch before I cycled home.

"It turned out to be a very good decision because I fell off my bicycle seven times on the way home."

EVERYONE can find it difficult making small talk with strangers at parties and business meetings. Former Edinburgh Fringe performer Cal Wilson from New Zealand recalled her most memorable encounter: "Once, as I started talking to a guy, I went to take a sip of my drink and the straw went straight up one nostril. I quickly lowered my glass, but the straw stayed in. He definitely noticed, because when I pulled the straw out, my nose started bleeding. In terms of getting his attention, it definitely worked a treat."

AS others see us. The American news network NBC has been discussing the introduction of minimum alcohol pricing in Scotland, and, after a detailed explanation of Scotland's difficulties with booze, it went out to pubs to get the reactions of punters. In the Abbotsford Bar in Rose Street, Edinburgh, NBC talked to Rhona, aged 50, who disagreed with First Minister Nicola Sturgeon's assessment that Scotland had an alcohol problem. "She had no right saying that. I don't think it's true," said Rhona. NBC then added the helpful description: "Rhona is with a bachelorette party drinking rum and Cokes. The bride-to-be, having drunk too much earlier, is back at the hotel already."

OUR whisky stories reminded George Maxwell in Lochgilphead of his younger brother, when 17, being an apprentice painter and having to work at a distillery in Dumbarton. Says George: "I got home to be told by our mother I should have seen the state of my brother who had come home the previous evening 'drunk as a monkey'.

"Turned out there was a pail of whisky at the distillery and everyone could help themselves by dipping a cup in. He told our mother his condition was caused by breathing in the fumes at the distillery, and our mother believed him."

As all mothers should.

HADN'T seen a colleague for a few days and assumed he had been snowed in at home. But he caught up with me yesterday to declare: "My dad's answer to everything was alcohol." After a suitable pause he added: "He didn't drink – he was just rubbish at quizzes."

9

I'll Vote for That

Politics seemed to be seeping into every corner of Scottish life, whether it was worries about Brexit, whether there should be a second independence referendum or what Trump was up to in America. Readers sent us their observations.

IRVINE Weavers held their annual meeting and dinner at the weekend when former MP Brian Donohoe recalled fellow Labour MP and Deputy Speaker Harold Walker once telling him that he was delivering leaflets at an election. It was shortly after a Tory canvasser had been too lazy to push the Tory leaflets right through the letterbox, so Harold would take them out and stuff them in his pocket.

Disaster struck when he arrived at one door and, looking round, realised that he had walked through the wet cement of a newly laid driveway. Harold quickly took a Tory leaflet out of his pocket, shoved it through the letterbox and made his escape.

AS worries continue about a hard Brexit, former Labour councillor Alan Stewart sees the news story about Prime Minister Theresa May welcoming the British cave divers who helped rescue the 12 boys in Thailand to Downing Street and asks: "Any chance of them getting us rescued from the dark, isolated, resourceless cavern that will be a Tory Brexit?" But some folk are trying to be positive. As Glasgow stand-up Frankie Boyle put it: "Boring to moan about the downside of Brexit. Let's focus on the exciting possibilities – living in an abandoned motorway services; coming up with a tasty recipe for fox; marrying a 3D-printed rifle; trading sexual favours for insulin, and vice versa – none of it will be dull."

FORMER Glasgow MP Tom Harris has resigned from the Labour Party. It reminds John Henderson: "In the late eighties when I was the Labour agent in affluent Bath, Ken Loach, the left-wing filmmaker of *Cathy Come Home* fame, decided to hold a press conference to renounce his party membership, as he felt Neil Kinnock was moving the party too much to the centre.

"The trouble was, I had to inform Loach and the press that it was a bit difficult for me to react to him leaving because, despite several written reminders, he hadn't paid his membership fees for three years, so technically he didn't have a membership to renounce."

AS many folk fear the worst if there is a hard Brexit, Russian Dmitri Grabov, now living in London, tries to be positive: "Don't let Project Fear scare you. I grew up with empty supermarkets and two-hour food queues in Moscow. Some days you got flour, other days you got cheese, maybe once a month you got sugar. The element of surprise made shopping incredibly exciting. You folks are in for a treat."

MUCH talk of protests when President Trump visits Scotland this month. Leo Kearse says: "Trump's unpopular in Scotland because they don't trust anyone who lives to 70."

STILL trying to understand American politics after President Trump backtracks on separating the children of illegal immigrants from their parents. His daughter Ivanka Trump praised her dad, stating: "Thank you, President, for taking critical action ending family separation at our border." But as Dan Pfeiffer replied to her: "You don't thank the kidnapper for releasing the hostages."

EVEN physicist and TV presenter Professor Brian Cox has entered the Brexit debate. As he memorably put it: "You can convince people to vote to abolish gravity, but they will be very p****d off with you when they hit the ground."

A READER sees the headline in *The Observer* 'Replace May with Gove' and gets in touch to say, "Tried it out. March, April, Gove, June, July. Nope, don't think it works."

SNP MP for Livingston Hannah Bardell was speaking at Westminster, where she said the Tory government was in a fankle over Brexit. The reporters at *Hansard*, which publishes Westminster debates, wrote to her asking: "The *Hansard* reporters would be grateful for the answer to the following specific query. Tangle? Fankle." Hannah was able to reassure them that "fankle" was a good Scottish word. It reminds us of when the late Tommy Graham, the rather gruff-speaking working-class Renfrewshire MP, spoke in Parliament. Not a word was understood by the poor *Hansard* staff who simply sent a request to Tommy to give them his written speech, which appeared in next day's *Hansard* verbatim.

SO what's been happening in England? A reader shows us an exchange on social media where a young woman reported: "Off tomorrow for Poland Day. Never heard of it." This prompted an angry chap to reply: "And we don't get a day off for St George's Day. What a joke this place is." Someone else wrote it was "pathetic" and another decried: "Nothing great about Britain these days."

Before the exchanges got even more heated, a friend added the explanation: "Are you sure it's not Polling Day, hun?"

GLASGOW stand-up Janey Godley received much publicity for holding up a very rude sign when Donald Trump last visited Scotland. It contained a word not used in respectable society. Anyway Janey has revealed: "Two Tories in my comedy gig tonight. Man smugly shouts, 'I hear you swear a lot. What's your worst word? Go on, let me hear it. We all know you are famous for saying it.' I reply, 'Foodbanks.' Audience cheers. Man sits raging."

IT'S the 20th anniversary of the Good Friday Agreement that brought peace to Northern Ireland. The late Mo Mowlam was Irish Secretary at the time, and we remember Mo at a book event in Glasgow years later telling us that she called her personal protection officers in Ireland "Shirleys". She went on to explain: "Whenever I suggested going anywhere remotely dodgy, they would always say to me, 'Shirley not, Minister.'" She also gave a talk at the Royal Concert Hall in Glasgow, where a woman in the audience gave her the very Glasgow compliment: "Mo, I enjoyed your talk more than I thought I would." She went on to ask for Mo's views on proportional representation, and Mo said she was all for it. The lady said: "I didn't enjoy your talk after all," and sat down.

LABOUR MSP Neil Findlay has launched his book *Socialism & Hope*, which has a foreword by party leader Jeremy Corbyn. Our attention is drawn, however, to a tale about the late great West Lothian MP Tam Dalyell, who once drove to a Labour Party conference with his breeks at his ankles. He confided to Neil it meant he arrived without his trousers being badly creased.

WE are still trying to make sense of the faltering Brexit negotiations. Quintin Forbes tries to help by rewriting an old saying: "Give a man a fish and he will eat for a day. Give a man a fishing rod and he is preparing for Brexit."

POLITICS in Britain is a bit mental just now. As Tory MP Anna Soubry said yesterday: "There must be something not quite right in your life when 45 minutes in a dentist's chair having a rather large root canal filling becomes a relaxing lie down and thinking time."

And it's not any better in America. Entertainer Bette Midler caustically put it: "This will be the first time a President looks exactly the same his whole time in office, while the rest of us visibly age due to the stress his lousy job puts us through."

THE original BBC news flash about that terrible poisoning of the former Russian spy said it had occurred in Sainsbury's, and not Salisbury, before it was changed. Says Patricia Watson: "It reminds me of when, at the height of The Beatles' fame, the BBC announced on the lunchtime news that Ringo Starr had had his toenails removed. By the Six O'Clock News the BBC was able to reassure the nation it was his tonsils that he had relinquished."

TSB chief executive Paul Pester is the latest business boss to go before a select committee of MPs and perform woefully, showing how little empathy he has for poor customers struggling with a botched IT system.

He told MPs that customers upset with the bank should use the bank's online complaint form rather than social media as "Everyone enjoys tweeting, but it is shouting into the void."

Says reader and TSB customer John Henderson: "As a

customer, I know the feeling Mr Pester – just like being put on indefinite hold on your TSB telephone helpline."

TALKING of MPs, many of them have taken to social media, but make comments that are dull, boring and unforgettable. So well done to the new Tory MP in Eastwood, Paul Masterton, who welcomed the sunny weather yesterday afternoon by declaring on Twitter: "Remember, on days like today, do your bit for humanity and check in on any ginger neighbours to make sure they have sufficient supplies of total block and a sun hat."

THE Herald reported that the Donald Trump-owned Turnberry Hotel has banned Irn-Bru. Reader Ian Barnett muses: "I cannot help thinking that The Donald believes it is actually called Iran Brew."

10

Head for the Sunshine

Away from work or the pub, readers have been enjoying their holidays, and they tell us when something happens to make them laugh.

EDINBURGH has been voted the top cruise-ship destination in Britain. It reminds us of the cruise-ship worker who told us he got a call at the ship's reception desk from an angry customer who said they had paid extra for a cabin with an ocean view but all they could see was a car park.

"We haven't sailed yet, sir," the crew member had to gently explain.

HOLIDAYMAKERS are now returning home, a little bit annoyed if they're being honest that the weather was so good in Scotland while they were away. Anyway, we are a bit sympathetic towards the young chap on a bus into Glasgow, overheard by a reader, who told a young woman who asked if he wanted to see her holiday pictures: "Unless you got attacked by a shark, then I'll pass."

And a Bearsden reader confides to us: "The wife packed her running gear saying she might go for a few early morning runs on holiday. That's the fifth year in a row she's done that. Never used it yet."

MONKEYS

Please close the Doors
& the Windows when
you leave the room

A BEARSDEN reader tells us she was at a dinner party where a doctor was loudly pontificating about his holidays before turning to his work and remarking that he had to put a patient into an induced coma. "What did you do?" asked a fellow dinner guest. "Tell him about your trip to India?"

YES, a sunny bank holiday in Scotland, which could only mean throngs of screeching teenagers invading Troon beach, and police being called to the first sailing of the season for that great paddle steamer *The Waverley* as too many folk had turned it into a booze cruise. Our mind wanders to the time when a crew member on *The Waverley* would occasionally perform the trick of catching a seagull by holding a piece of bread over the deck-rail and grabbing it by its feet. He would then march past startled passengers to the galley, shouting: "Chef, I've got that extra chicken you needed."

LOTS of tourists about. David Russell tells us he and a pal arrived at an Edinburgh bus stop where two Australian girls were studying the printed timetable. Says David: "We stood behind them and, shielding our eyes from the sun's glare, checked the digital 'real-time' board which sits on an adjacent, higher pole. 'Next one is not for 20 minutes,' we told them. The girls looked at us askance. 'How can you tell just by looking at the sky?' one asked."

TALKING of authors, many of us can identify with writer Jill Mansell, who was telling folk: "Just spent ages booking a holiday apartment online. It then flashed up that the place was no longer available. I was furious for an hour, until I realised it was no longer available because I'd booked it."

OUR tales of B&Bs remind Willie McLean in Dumbarton: "Two driving examiners sent to a Scottish island were staying at a large guest house in the attic bedrooms. The rooms were not en suite, and when they retired for the night they realised the toilets were on the ground floor. One of them decided that rather than go down and back up three flights of stairs he would do the necessary from the attic window. At breakfast they complimented the owner on the quality of the tea, and he told them, 'I tell my clients that it's not the tea, it's the water. We use the rainwater from the roof, which we collect in the big butt in the garden.'"

QUITE a small subset of Diary stories, but nonetheless our tale of having to wee out of a B&B attic window reminds Ken Johnson: "When I was a lot younger I woke in an attic room with an urgent need. I knew there was a toilet on that floor but couldn't remember which door, so the window in the gable beckoned. A terrible rattling sound was heard and I realised that there was an outhouse below with a corrugated iron roof. Stopping was not an option, so I had to carry on, hoping no one would hear the racket. When someone remarked to the landlady at breakfast that they heard heavy rain overnight, she said that the ground was dry. Maybe it was my imagination but I thought she was looking at me as she said it."

WE mentioned it was National B&B Day tomorrow, and a reader recalls the late Donald Dewar, when First Minister, speaking at a dinner where he said he was staying at a B&B where the honey was served at breakfast in a tiny jar. Donald said he couldn't resist using the Chic Murray line to the owner: "I see you keep a bee."

JOHN Parker adds to our B&B stories: "In the late eighties Coatbridge teens travelled to Blackpool for the September weekend and the chance of a hedonistic time.

"On arrival at the B&B that promised us a beachfront view, we were led to a dingy room that was sub-divided with gyprock into ever smaller spaces.

"One safety-minded friend asked where the fire escape was and was directed to a window with a rope snaking out, tied to a radiator below the window.

"The landlady said, 'Be careful, boys and girls – one at a time down the rope.'"

BUS tours, a story. Kate Woods, now in America, tells us: "One of my male relatives was given a 'stag' bus trip in Scotland, visiting many pubs up the west coast with his male friends. As the coach was driving up the side of Loch Awe, the driver said that usually he drove groups of elderly holidaymakers and as he had an all-male group he was going to give the information that he always wanted to give. He then switched to his tour-guide voice and said if the passengers would look out the left-hand side they would see the magnificent and scenic Loch Awe. He then added, 'And, gentlemen, if you now look out the right-hand side you will be greeted with a wonderful view of 'F*** Awe'."

WE mentioned the dwindling art of sending postcards and Robert Gardner tells us: "My first holiday abroad was at a

Scout Jamboree in Greece when I was 16. I had been told that a postcard was expected, and after a few days I sent one packed with information about how I was getting on and so on. When I got home there was the card marked out of 10 for punctuation and grammar. From then on postcards were sent with one word only – 'Fine'."

MUSICIAN Roy Gullane adds to our B&B stories by telling us: "A fellow performer, finding himself peckish after a show, managed to grope his way through the darkened house into the kitchen. He could see nothing edible except a huge 40lb block of cheddar cheese, into which he plunged the only available cutting tool, a rather large steak knife. He was just about to liberate a goodly chunk when a voice boomed out behind him, 'What do you think you're doing?' Slightly flustered, our hero looked at the B&B proprietor, back to the cheese and knife, and said, 'Whoever pulls it out gets to be king.'"

WE asked for your postcard stories before they disappear, and Robin Gilmour in Milngavie tells us about the chap who sent his girlfriend a postcard with a bathing beauty on the front. When he got home he had some explaining to do as when writing "Wish you were here" on the back, he missed out the last letter.

GOING on holiday can be stressful. Mount Vernon reader Maureen Lanigan tells us her brother John was in a Greggs in

Hastings when a wee Scottish woman behind him asked for a pie. When the assistant asked what kind, and she replied, "A Scotch pie!" the girl asked what that was.

"A wee roon' pie wae mince in it!" replied the shocked customer, and John had to tell her they didn't do them down in Hastings. "But it's Greggs!" the perplexed woman replied. "They must do them!" Before adding: "What are we going to eat!"

BUS tours, continued. Says Willie McLean in Dumbarton: "Some years ago while on a bus tour in Dublin, we were passing the Guinness Brewery and the hostess told us the story about Arthur Guinness. He married his wife Olivia in 1761 and they had 21 children. Sadly only 10 survived to adulthood. We were told Olivia was hard of hearing and when retiring at night Arthur would say, 'Are we going to sleep or what?' Olivia would frequently reply, 'What?' The rest is history."

TOUR buses, continued. If you have ever visited Lewis, you might have seen the 20-foot-high whalebone arch at Bragar which is formed from the jawbones of a blue whale. A reader tells us: "The late Iain Morrison provided tours around the island, often for passengers off cruise ships. When he approached Bragar he would begin an account of a family having an exceptionally large turkey at Christmas. It was, according to Iain, large enough to feed everyone in the village. When the bus came round the last bend and into full sight of the arch, he explained to the bemused passengers that it was the wishbone of the mythical turkey."

OUR story about midges reminds Roddy Young of staying at a lodge in Dalavich, Argyll and Bute, last summer when he had a look in the guest book. Someone had written: "We all had a good stay. Very enjoyable. Except for midgets!" Roddy felt that seemed a bit harsh.

BUS tours, continued. John Barrington writes: "A while ago, one of the tour-bus drivers, who frequented Inversnaid Hotel, was renowned for pointing out places of interest to his passengers, mostly people from south of Hadrian's Wall.

"His particular passion seemed to be ancient battlefields; here the hillside where the Scots beat the Auld Enemy, there the field where the Scots triumphed over the Auld Enemy. And so on, day after day.

"Towards the end of one particular holiday, a visitor spoke up, saying that, from his now-rather-distant schooldays, he could remember the teacher telling of an occasional English victory over the Scots. This met with the instant rejoinder, 'No' on my bus, they didn't!'"

CONGRATULATIONS to David Keat at the Brander Lodge Hotel near Oban, who got himself lots of publicity by saying he would serve burgers coated in a midge dressing. It reminds us of the English tourist who was complaining about being bitten by midges at a Scottish tearoom and a customer advising her that she should try midge nets, which were sold in the shop next door. "Are they difficult to catch?" she asked.

AMERICANS – we really do love them. Scottish band the Tannahill Weavers are on a tour of the States just now and were playing in Wisconsin the other night. Says band member Roy Gullane: "At the après-show 'meet 'n' greet' I was informed by an older lady (ages wi' masel') that she had visited Edinburgh many years ago. 'Do they still have the castle?' she enquired. I was going to tell her it was now an IKEA but didn't like to burst her bubble."

BUS tours, continued. Says John Anderson in Bishopton: "I am a tour guide and I was with a group of American tourists at the Rest and Be Thankful viewpoint. Looking at the surrounding hills one of them asked me, 'Do they mow the grass round here?'"

TRAVELLERS often ask website TripAdvisor for help, and a 19-year-old from Boston in the US wrote this week: "Hey there! I'm going to Glasgow and was wondering if there was any way I can make some friends. My friends, who were supposed to go with me, told me they don't want to go any more, so I'm flying solo."

After various suggestions about pubs, tours, cafes and so on, a chap who calls himself Mad Scotsman astutely replied: "Stand at a bus stop and mention the weather."

OUR tales of tourists remind David Russell in Penicuik of a local building a house, who was wearing a T-shirt with "Sheriff" printed within a star on the front and carrying a long-handled axe he had just bought in a hardware store. Says David: "Bearded, and looking a bit like Grizzly Adams, he walked down the main street only to be accosted by a passing American tourist driving a camper van. 'Excuse me officer, is this the route to Edinburg?' After giving the colonial cousin directions he wondered what this guy thought Scottish cops actually looked like."

COULDN'T believe how red a colleague's face has become with all this sunny weather.

He saw me staring so came over to tell me: "I saw a sign in a shop 'Midge nets £10'. I didn't even know insects could play the lottery."

To the person who stole my 4 year old grandaughters paddling pool, I hope you drown in it

WE turn to holiday site TripAdvisor, where the Wallace Monument near Stirling gets hundreds of enthusiastic reviews, and one negative remark where a visitor from Oaxaca, Mexico, states: "We decided not to pay the entrance fee and waited for our companions in the Keeper's Lodge. We were initially delighted to be provided with a charming colouring page featuring a kilt-clad bear, but from this point on, our visit took a severe turn for the worse.

"We were exceptionally disappointed by the monument's upkeep of their coloured pencil supplies. Not only were the vast majority dull to the point of dysfunction, they were utterly lacking in pigmentation. I would warn any future visitors against high expectations for the coloured pencil offerings at this location."

Wallace Monument staff replied that they have now sharpened the pencils.

AH, the Scottish accent. Donald Grant tells us: "My family and I are down in Hampshire, and while visiting the village pub for lunch, the bar lady confided in me how much she enjoyed hearing a Scottish accent again.

"She whispered that several years ago she had met a Scot and his accent made her go all weak at the knees every time that she had gone out with him – but she had to give him up. Her answer to my questioning look was not what I had expected: 'My husband found out.'"

11

Travel Broadens the Mind

Travel can be a stressful time. But where there is stress there is often humour. Here are our readers' tales from when they go out and about.

STRESSFUL time, going on holiday. As Paddy Galloway recorded on his way to Portugal: "Scenes in Dublin Airport as a red-faced man shouts at his wife for losing the passports. 'You remembered every ******* pair of shoes but not the ******* passports' has been the standout line."

LOTS of folk using the Uber app in Glasgow to summon cabs. But it does have the occasional drawback. A reader in the city centre at the weekend heard a young woman who was staring at her phone ask her pal: "A Nissan Pulsar Acenta? Who the heck knows what that looks like?"

A COLLEAGUE comes over to tell us: "I've discovered a cure for my fear of flying – 23 hours on a National Express coach."

AN Ayrshire reader tells us: "Sometimes you forget how proud you can feel to be Scottish." He was chatting to a work colleague in England who had been in the Royal Navy for 20 years and he asked him if he had ever seen any action. Adds our reader: "Totally straight-faced he told me, 'The guy next to me went down to gunfire once, that was the closest.' When I asked where, he told me in the eighties HMS *London* sailed up the Clyde on a Friday night and, as the crew took to the deck to see the city lights, the sailor next to him was struck on the shoulder by a shot fired by a gang of neds on the embankment with an air rifle."

WE are all a bit afraid of saying anything challenging to flight crew these days, as you sense they are ready at a moment's notice to call security. So a reader flying down to London from Glasgow was impressed when a chap using his phone to play games while the plane stood on the tarmac was told by a steward to put his phone on airplane mode and the chap replied: "We've been sitting here for half an hour – is it not time to put the plane in airplane mode?'"

WE mentioned Chic Murray gags, and thank you to readers who sent in their favourites. Sadly we've printed most of them before, but one I hadn't heard came from John Mathieson, who says: "I liked his comment on the compensation culture where individuals took advantage of deficiencies in the performance of public services. As a schoolboy he was on the top deck of a bus with his father when the bus performed a very abrupt emergency stop. Passengers were thrown forwards, and Chic said, 'I was uninjured, but fortunately my father had the presence of mind to throw me down the stairs.'"

WE asked about stressful airport moments and a reader in America tells us of a team from the US flying to the World Irish Dance Championships in Glasgow last year who were carrying their expensive dance dresses in suit bags as well as their normal carry-on luggage. An officious airline staff member insisted they check them into the hold, which the girls resisted, fearing damage. After a hurried consultation the girls came up with the idea of putting the dresses on over their normal clothes, stuffed the empty suit bags in their hand luggage, then changed out of them once on the plane. The official was no doubt hopping mad.

WE do love bus drivers. Sue Wade in Ayr was at her local bus station when she heard a passenger ask the driver: "How long to get to Hamilton?"

"Ages," he replied.

GOOD to see sexism being challenged. Sandy Tuckerman recalls: "On a late-night flight from London Gatwick, in the days before the flight-deck doors were locked and bolted, the announcement was, 'Ten minutes to landing, wenches on the benches.'

"The senior flight attendant stormed into the cockpit, slamming the door behind her. A rather contrite announcement was then made by the captain: 'I do apologise, ladies and gentlemen. What I meant to say was, cabin crew, seats for landing.'"

YES, it's Easter this weekend, but that doesn't mean all the parking meters in Glasgow are free to use. We remember a reader going back to his car on an Easter Monday and, seeing it was being ticketed, he remonstrated with the warden that it was a bank holiday. "It's no' a bank holiday for me, pal," he replied, and kept on writing.

AH yes, public transport. We can sympathise with artist Moose Allain who says: "The old lady sitting near me on this train must have seen some things in her lifetime, have so many amazing tales to tell. Unfortunately, the one she's been telling for the last half an hour isn't one of them."

OUR story about breakfast in Glasgow reminds former BBC producer Mike Shaw of the late great folk singer Danny Kyle once telling him about travelling overnight to Glasgow after a gig in the north of England and being desperate for breakfast.

Although it was five in the morning Danny spotted a greasy spoon that was open, rushed in and ordered a full breakfast and a cup of coffee.

When the coffee arrived he took a large gulp and smilingly told the waitress it tasted like nectar.

"Well, if you don't like it, you don't have to drink it," she replied.

A LATE-ARRIVING-TRAIN story, with Mark Boyle in Johnstone telling us: "During the recent snow, ScotRail blared over the tannoy at Johnstone that, during the rush hour, trains would be up to half an hour late, subject to cancellation at short notice and accommodation inside carriages would be standing room only. I wonder where to thank them for the improved service?"

A REFLECTION on life at Glasgow Airport. A reader passing through the security area hears the official ask a passenger just before she goes through the metal detector if she has anything in her pockets. "No," she replied.

"I know how that feels," he replies ruefully.

BUS stories, continued. Says Mary Duncan: "One morning on my way to work there was a passenger singing like a linty, happily drunk. He got off the bus just before me, and when I moved to the front I said to the driver, 'How can someone be that drunk at eight in the morning?' The driver's reply: 'Just lucky, I guess.'"

TODAY'S piece of sheer daftness comes from Chris Addison, who says: "Well, turns out when they say at the station, 'If you see anything suspicious please report it to a member of staff,' they don't mean those posters claiming 97 per cent of the trains last month were on time."

GERMAN newspapers reported that the Berlin Wall has now been down longer than it actually existed, if you can follow that arithmetical conundrum. It reminds us of the Scottish doctor who told us about being at a medical conference in Berlin in the eighties where a local medic took him to see the wall. He told us: "Directly opposite was a tower with an East German armed guard. Between us and the wall was a fence, then a no-man's-land of bare ground. Directly under the guard, written on the wall was 'Gers Ya Bass'.

"I started laughing. My German friend asked what was so

amusing, and I explained. He was dumbfounded. 'You mean that someone risked his life to write a football slogan on this wall, where so many have been shot? This has been on the wall for a year – we had no idea what it meant, or even the language it was in.'"

THE railways folk have announced you will no longer be able to share a sleeper carriage between London and Glasgow with a stranger, which was a way of saving yourself 50 quid or so. We always remember our late, great colleague Willie Hunter's description of sharing a sleeper back to Glasgow after watching Scotland beat the world champions at Wembley in 1967. Wrote Willie: "After taking a refreshment, I fell on to the top bunk of a train sleeper from Euston. At wakey-wakey time the mouth felt like the inside of Jim Baxter's stockings.

"Silently, over the rim of the bed appeared a bottle of Irn-Bru. With my provident companion from downstairs, who turned out to be a van driver and a Clyde supporter, there was a happy hour of living the triumph all over again, while we took our mornings of his Bru and what we could find in our half-bottles."

OUR bus stories remind Ronnie McLean of working as an SMT bus conductor as a student in the sixties. He recalls: "Running late on a trip to Killermont Street, we stopped at lights on Cathedral Street and the driver told me to change the destination blind so we could make a quick getaway. While I was hanging on to the front of the bus – a Bristol Lodekka for the anoraks – the lights changed and he drove off with me clinging on. Typical of Glasgow, no one in the crowded bus station batted an eyelid."

AND talking of tramcars, enough readers to fill a tramcar have got in touch with the classic tale, so I suppose we should repeat it, of the greyhound owner outside Shawfield trying to get on a tramcar with two dugs but being told by the clippie that there was already a dog on board and only two were allowed in total.

After a long and heated argument in which the conductress would not bend the rules, he eventually stormed off in anger, shouting at her: "You can stick your caur up your backside."

She merely shouted back: "Aye, if you'd done that with wan o' yer dugs, you would've got oan."

WE mentioned the reduction of postcards these days, and Martin McGeehan in Gourock recalls a school trip to St Malo in the sixties which was the first trip abroad for most of them. Says Martin: "We were tasked on day one with buying a postcard and stamp to send news of our arrival and comfortable accommodation to home. A pal addressed his card to his family at 'Rue de Forsyth, Greenock' so that 'the French postman would know where to deliver it'."

THE Herald archive picture of a burned-down Glasgow theatre reminds David Miller in Milngavie of another Glasgow theatre consumed by fire, the old Queen's Theatre. Says David: "The theatre's resident comic Sammy Murray was on a tram and asked the conductress, 'Does this caur go over Jamaica Street Bridge?'

"'If it disnae,' she replied, 'there's gonna be a hell of a splash.'"

BIT of a stooshie on social media as our old chum, writer and broadcaster Lesley Riddoch, commented: "Arriving in Glasgow, every person leaving bus thanks the driver. Such a contrast from impersonal silence at Stansted." SNP MSP Roseanna Cunningham agreed with her, stating:

"Used to do that in London to bus drivers – they always looked shocked that anyone would thank them!" Many others, though, said that thanking bus drivers happened all over Britain, and people in Scotland should be less sanctimonious.

But the most searing reply was the chap who told Lesley: "I held the door open for you in Starbucks, The Gyle. You were walking with a stick and holding a coffee. Not much of a thanks was forthcoming."

OUR bus stories brought back memories for entertainer Andy Cameron, who was a bus conductor in the early sixties. Says Andy: "When passengers had no money for their fare they could ask for a Pink Slip on which they wrote their names and addresses so that they could go to the Bath Street office and pay it later. What always surprised me was the number of famous people who lived in Castlemilk and were skint – Rock Hudson, Perry Como, Willie Henderson, Paddy Crerand, Harold Wilson, Marilyn Monroe – they were all on my bus and signed a Pink Slip."

OK, just to get it over with. We mentioned the classic tram-car story about the two dogs and now numerous readers demand we mention the other classic tram tale. We will use Ian Cooper of Bearsden's version: "A Glasgow wifie purchased an old metal cabin trunk at The Barras and, as was the custom then, she put it up front with the driver of a tram on the Gallowgate then went to board herself, only to be told by the clippie that the car was fu'.

"'But I'm the woman wi' the tin chest,' she cried.

"'Ah don't care if ye've goat a wally erse, you're still no' gettin' on!' she was told."

A CUMBERNAULD reader emails to tell us: "With the possibility growing of self-driving vehicles, it's only a matter of time before we get a country and western song where a guy's truck leaves him too."

LATE night in Glasgow and we jump into a taxi and recognise the driver.

"Is your brother still driving your taxi during the day?" we ask.

"No, I had to sack him," says our driver.

"Why was that?" we ask. "Well, despite what experts say, his passengers didn't like it when he tried to go the extra mile."

THE *Herald* story about Scots spending a large portion of their salary on train fares has a Glasgow reader getting in touch to say: "I got an early morning train from Glasgow to Edinburgh which was so full many folk were standing. The chap who managed to get a seat beside me remarked, 'It's kind of sad that getting a seat on the train will probably be the highlight of my day, and I'll be talking about it when I get home.'"

WE mentioned the 30th anniversary this week of the opening of the Glasgow Garden Festival, and Margaret Thomson recalls: "A friend of mature years visited the festival and decided she had to go on the Coca-Cola ride. When she landed, we asked how she had enjoyed it. 'Well,' she said, 'it was OK, but I had one hand clapped over my eyes to keep my specs on, and the other over my mouth to keep my teeth in, so I didn't see much.'"

CONGRATULATIONS to my old chum, and the journalist who took The Diary to giddy heights, Tom Shields, for his lifetime achievement award at the Scottish Press Awards. Tom is remembered by readers for his Diary stories poking gentle fun at the Ayrshire town of Kilwinning. He once wrote about the Kilwinning chap who announced he was getting married and his pal warning him: "No her! Hauf the men in Stevenston huv been wi' her!" After a moment's thought he replied philosophically: "Ach, it's no that big a place, Stevenston."

COMEDIAN Brian "Limmy" Limond, who will be in Inverness this month with his video clip tour, Limmy's Vines, explained to followers on social media what happened when he encountered the £2 drop-off fee at Glasgow Airport.

Said Limmy: "Glasgow Airport charges two quid just to drop somebody off. Got an Uber there and saw the sign, so I tipped the driver two quid to make up for it. Checked my receipt, and saw he'd added the two quid charge anyway. It's dog-eat-dog. You know where you are? You're in the jungle, baby."

12

The Funny Side of the Law

Even finding yourself in front of a police officer or in a court can have its lighter moments.

BIG problem in Scottish prisons just now is the number of hidden mobile phones. A reader was speaking to a prison officer who told him that the prison received a phone call from a mother asking if they could pass on a message to her son. Says our reader: "The officer asked what the message was and she replied, 'Tell him I've put £20 credit on his phone.' The officer then asked, 'What number did you add the credit to?' and the innocent woman rattled off the mobile-phone number. The officer then walked to the prisoner's closed cell door, took out his own phone and dialled the number. At a 'hullo', he opened the door and met the gaze of the bemused felon, then duly confiscated the illicit device."

A READER hears a chap in his Ayrshire golf club at the weekend tell fellow players: "I got stopped by the police and the officer asked me if I knew why he had pulled me over.

"I just replied, 'Well, I have a few ideas, but I'd like to hear your suggestion first.'"

A GLASGOW reader hears a young chap in his pub announce: "Glasgow City Council sent me a photograph of my car in a bus lane, and they wanted 60 quid for it. I sent it back though – it was way too expensive and the quality was really bad."

WE commiserate with a former colleague who has had his car nicked. One of his pals tells him: "My dad once had his car stolen with hundreds of pounds worth of fishing equipment in the back.

"The car turned up a few miles away with the fishing equipment untouched and a note to say, 'Sorry, I just couldn't walk any further.'"

A GLASGOW lawyer tells us of a colleague representing a client in a divorce case and how he had asked her to write down her income and outgoings.

At the end, where she wrote what she had left over every month, she had simply put "F.A."

When he stood up and told the sheriff that she had absolutely no income left when the bills were paid his client looked confused and whispered to him: "Family allowance."

A READER in Hyndland emails us with some safety advice: "You should never text while you are driving. All it takes is one moment of distraction and suddenly everyone in the group chat thinks you can't spell."

GOOD to see Police Scotland launching a campaign against bogus callers arriving at your doorstep. It, of course, reminds us of the classic tale of the Glasgow officer arriving at the door of an old lady in a Maryhill tenement who refused to open her door, shouting: "How do I know you're the polis?" The officer bent down so that he could show her his warrant card through the letter box. The flap opened and a pair of eyes stared out. It then rapidly closed, and the old woman yelled: "Away, ya bugger … ye don't get polis that wee."

REMEMBER your nervousness when you had to sit your driving test? A young West of Scotland chap remarked on social media the other day: "My driving instructor said to me, 'Are you just back fae Tenerife?' and I went, 'Naw, just the sun beds.'

"And then he said, 'No, it's because you're on the wrong side of the road.'"

OUR tale about Led Zeppelin reminds David Russell: "As a rookie cop I attended Edinburgh's Carlton Hotel in the seventies with an older cop following a report of excessive noise from a suite.

"We found an after-gig party by mega rockers Deep Purple in full flow. 'Turn the noise down, son!' said the older officer.

"'But we're Deep Purple!'

"'I don't care whit colour you are, son. Turn it down or somebody's getting lifted,' he replied."

THE wit of our sheriffs in Scotland is often overlooked.

Lawyer Brian Chrystal was reading a case report and tells us: "Just to show that the spirit of PG Wodehouse and Rumpole has not completely died in our legal system, the Sheriff, required to assess the reliability of an expert witness, wrote that 'the witness treated cross-examination in the manner a man might hold a crocodile'." Snappy.

TALKING of false teeth – as we do sometimes in The Diary – an East Kilbride reader tells us that when he worked in a Coatbridge bar years ago a regular came in and said he had been kept in the police station overnight after a misdemeanour.

When he was allowed to go, and handed his belongings, he noticed he had lost his false teeth and asked where they were. Says our reader: "The desk sergeant rummaged below the desk and came up with a box containing a large number of sets of false teeth and told him, 'Take your pick.' My customer had a look but decided just to leave it."

A GLASGOW lawyer swears to us that a potential juror at a Sheriff Court trial said he could not be off his work for the week that the trial was expected to take. The Sheriff asked: "Can't they do without you?" and the juror replied: "Yes, but I don't want them to know that."

YES, the barbecues are being well used in Scotland just now. Hugh Walsh in Dalry tells us: "Enjoying a walk down Ayr High Street, I overheard the following conversation from two ladies. 'Did you enjoy the barbecue, Jeanie?'

"'Aye, but some b****** stole my bottle of gin.'

"'Was that the gin you bought from the shoplifter?'"

Says Hugh: "Just shows, you can't trust anyone these days."

AFTER the news story about police officers being taken to the island of Lismore after the first housebreaking in living memory, reader John Marshall in Auchtermuchty recalls: "In the early sixties we spent a long day on Lismore, and my father went into the phone box to contact the Appin ferryman to get an earlier crossing. He came out to say there was a full bottle of whisky on the shelf. When he quizzed the ferryman, he was told that when a local ran dry he would phone the mainland, the ferryman left the bottle and he would collect and pay later. 'We are all honest here,' he said. 'There is no thieving on Lismore.'"

13

Retail Therapy

Shops are having a difficult time keeping their customers as the internet takes its toll, but our readers can still raise a smile when they venture out on the high streets with their bags for life.

AN EDINBURGH reader tells us: "I went into a cafe the other day and there was a sign on the counter which said, 'We have no Wi-Fi. Pretend it's like the old days'. So I gave them 40p for my coffee and lit up a fag. Apparently that's not what they meant."

RESTAURANT chain Wimpy has plans to expand after years of cutbacks, and we wonder if they will reopen in Glasgow, as Wimpy was the first place many older Glaswegians first had a coffee outside their home. A reader once told us that he went into a Wimpy which had a sign stating "Free fried egg with every order", as it was hoping this would enhance folks' dining experience. He thought nothing of it, as he was only in for a takeaway coffee, but as he was leaving he was handed a brown paper bag – and, yes, the fried egg was inside it.

NOT everyone is getting into the swing of the new trendy coffee shops. A reader in one such establishment in Glasgow's Finnieston heard the bearded barista ask the old chap in front who had asked for a coffee if he wanted regular coffee or decaffeinated. The old chap sighed and replied: "What do you think? Do you want me to pay in real money or Monopoly money?"

A WEST END reader tells us that one of her girlfriends has admitted that her new boyfriend is not that bright after she told him she liked her steaks rare and he replied: "What? Like kangaroo or bison?"

A READER in a Glasgow restaurant the other night heard a woman at the next table order a complicated dessert, and the waiter explained: "Just to let you know, it will take 20 minutes to prepare."

"So why are you still standing here?" she replied.

"IT was so cold the other day," a Hamilton reader phones to tell us: "A woman buying fags in a corner shop was wearing two pairs of pyjamas."

A NEWTON MEARNS reader tells us he heard a shopper in the supermarket ask for a specific brand of vinaigrette dressing and was told it was out of stock. The chap then asked the assistant: "Any chance you could give me a note for the wife stating that I had looked everywhere for it and couldn't find it?"

WHAT larks when cheap and cheerful supermarket Lidl announced it was taking over the premises of the former upmarket Whole Foods Market in aspirational Giffnock, and folk were making fun of the supposed alarm in the minds of Giffnockians fearing their enclave on Glasgow's Southside was going downhill. Our favourite reaction on social media was Jploughownes, who declared: "Giffnock punters going tonto about a Lidl being built. Wait until the first time they go down the fourth aisle and come out with a four-man tent, a cutlery set, a Swiss army axe and a pair of long johns wae trainers built into them, aw for about six quid."

SHOP assistant banter, continued. Says John Mathieson: "Last year an English friend was accompanying me to a Burns Supper, and in a show of solidarity decided to wear an item of Scottish clothing. He drew the line at wearing a kilt.

"He went into a gents' outfitters in north Northumberland and asked the assistant, 'Do you have any Scottish ties?' and the assistant replied, 'Yes, I've got an auntie in Auchtermuchty.'"

MATT Vallance in Ayrshire passes on the drama of a fellow Ayrshireman who revealed on social media: "Some guy in Greggs in Cumnock moaning about his sausage roll being 'stane caul'. Handed it back to the woman to feel it through the paper bag, and she's like, 'Aye it will be stane caul – that's yer eclair.'"

A PARTICK reader swears to us that he was at his local supermarket, and when the bill for his messages came to

£20 exactly he told the checkout operator, as he fished in his pocket: "That's a nice round figure." She replied: "You're not so thin yourself."

IT'S great that Glasgow is such a multicultural city these days but sometimes acceptable social behaviour can vary. A Strathbungo reader tells us: "I was in a big department store having my make-up checked by one of the staff at the beauty counter.

"She was from Hong Kong and was perhaps a bit more outspoken than we are used to, as she looked at my face and declared: "You fat face! You need blusher! Blusher for fat face."

IT was reported yesterday that chocolate manufacturer Nestlé had failed in its bid at the European Court of Justice to have the four-finger shape of a Kit Kat registered as a trademark. We are indebted to Tom White, who tells us that the noise of a Kit Kat being snapped in their television advert was actually created by snapping a stalk of frozen celery. And a reader phones with a Kit Kat joke: "Guy goes to the window of a late-night garage on his way home from the pub and asks the girl behind the Perspex, 'Can I have a Kit Kat Chunky?'

"'Not if you're going to call me names,' she replied."

DOING your bit for the environment can be tricky. A reader in a Glasgow cafe heard an auld fella question a sign on the counter saying that plastic straws were now banned. "We have to keep them out of the ocean," the young girl behind the counter earnestly explained when he asked.

"Why's that?" replied the old chap. "Are they worried about a shark wi' a moothful o' straws sucking the blood out of some swimmer?"

WHO doesn't want an ice cream in this sunny weather? But, as Gerry McBride confesses: "Me: 'I'll have a 99 please.' Ice-cream man: 'Syrup?' Me: 'What have you got?' Ice-cream man: 'Chocolate or strawberry.' Me: 'Eh, how about the green one?' Ice-cream man: 'That's antibacterial handwash.'"

THE barbecues are wafting their rich aromas over the sub-
urbs just now. A Bishopbriggs reader was at a neighbour's
the other night when a fellow invited neighbour came down
the path and said: "I've brought some vegetarian kebabs.
Where will I put them?" The chap flipping the burgers
merely replied: "I think the bin's over to your left."

A GLASGOW reader was in a Maryhill supermarket when
he heard the customer being asked: "How many bags would
you like?" The old fella replied: "No idea. Why don't we put
the messages in bags until we have no messages left and that's
the number of bags."

NO idea why, but someone has decreed that it is British
Sandwich Week. We wonder if there is a better-named
sandwich shop than the one a reader spotted in Bondi,
Sydney, entitled "How the Focaccia?" Anyway, Duncan
Cameron once told us of being on a trade mission in New
York where a Glaswegian in the party went into a deli for
a sandwich and the New Yorker behind the counter went
into overdrive listing all the available breads. When he finally
finished his litany of rye, wholemeal, bagel, ciabatta and so
on, she replied: "Jist whatever you've got open, son."

SUSAN Irvine in Penicuik tells us: "A friend once lived with
her family in Mexico where, at a ladies' gathering hosted by
her mother, the dainty edging of the little puff pastries was

much admired. Curious to know the secret of such a fine finish, the party visited the kitchen down in the basement where the cook Maria, flattered by the attention, was pleased to demonstrate.

She closed the dough around the fillings, then whipped out the top set of her dentures to seal the pastry's edges. Simple!" And with that we really must put our false-teeth stories away on the bathroom shelf.

YES, many of us welcomed the sugar tax that led to the makers of Irn-Bru reducing the sugar content of their drink. But as Amna, whose dad runs a local store in Glasgow, was telling friends yesterday: "My favourite thing is being told that folk are going into my dad's shop asking if he's got any of the 'good stuff in the back' because they heard he still has some old-recipe Irn-Bru kicking about."

A READER back from holiday in America commends an item on the menu in a diner he ate at which he feels would prove popular back here.

He tells us: "Under 'Extras' on the menu was an item called 'My girlfriend is not hungry'. For an extra $3, if you order this item, the kitchen doubles the amount of chips they serve you with your burger and adds three extra onion rings."

A P.A. named Pamela emails to tell us it's National Tea Day later this month, whatever that may be. It does, though, remind us of the Kelvin Hall staff member who was explaining to an underling the art of tea-making in an urn. The trick it seems is to put in four tea bags for each gallon of water, so that a four-gallon urn should have 16 tea bags.

"And how do we know when it's ready?" asked the younger member of staff.

"Simple," said the older one. "What we do now is go for a fag, and when we are finished, the tea will be ready."

THE recent shortages of fruit and veg in the supermarkets remind Michael McGeachy of when he was a supermarket manager in Fife and the pineapples were delivered with small sachets of moisture-absorption pellets. The store's telephonist asked what they were and was told they were pineapple seeds, so she popped one in a pot and put it on the windowsill, where she regularly watered it.

Says Michael: "After a few weeks with nothing growing, I cut the top leaves off a pineapple and placed them into the pot, tips protruding from the soil, and she was so excited. Week by week we ensured the leaves grew bigger. We were rumbled when a visitor knocked over the pot, which fell on to the floor, and a rather sorry-looking pineapple top rolled under her desk. I never knew such a polite lady could know so many swear words."

THEY are ubiquitous, so it was perhaps inevitable that a Specsavers shop, a Lloyds Pharmacy and a Greggs are next door to each other in Kings Heath High Street in Birmingham.

"Locals are referring to the shops as 'Specs and drugs and sausage rolls'."

IT seems a few folk are agitated about the trendy American food store Whole Foods in Giffnock announcing its closure – more than 1,500 people have signed an online petition opposing the shutdown. Pity they didn't use it a bit more often. Anyway it reminds us of the story, which we listed under apocryphal, summing up the store's perceived pretentiousness. It was the customer at the Whole Foods checkout who declared: "I need to read the numbers on the barcode out to you – I don't want any lasers touching my food."

A READER in Hyndland emails the thought-provoking: "I just want to be rich enough to throw leftovers after dinner straight into the bin rather than putting them in a plastic tub in the fridge for a week and then throwing them out."

THE news pages report that the men involved in the annual hunt for gugas – young gannets – have received threats that police are investigating. Eating the gugas is not to everyone's taste. As a reader once told us: "A wizened islander said that once on Mingulay, while looking after sheep, he and his mates tried a guga, or 'Barra duck' as it's known. 'The guga wasn't very nice, so we gave it to the dog,' said the old man in his soft lilting brogue, 'but he had to lick his backside to get the taste of it out his mouth.'"

OUR cafe stories remind our contact at the Royal Scottish National Orchestra: "Moons ago a string quartet from the RSNO was despatched from Glasgow to promote the orchestra's forthcoming season. At a break in performances, they stopped for lunch at a hostelry in rural Angus. Having scanned the menu, one of the musicians asked the attentive, though perhaps inexperienced, waitress what the 'soupe du jour' was. Endeavouring to find out, the waitress returned triumphantly from the kitchens to declare that it was, in fact, the Soup of the Day."

MANY of us will have experienced this problem when buying something online from Amazon. Writes a reader: "Dear

Amazon, I bought a toilet seat because I needed one. Necessity, not desire. I do not collect them. I am not a toilet seat addict. No matter how temptingly you email me, I'm not going to think, oh go on then, just one more toilet seat, I'll treat myself."

TODAY'S piece of whimsy comes from Ian Power who declares: "Studies have shown that food tastes about 40 per cent better if it's eaten whilst your other hand is holding open the fridge door."

OUR B&Q story prompts entertainer Andy Cameron to recount the – no, not old, but shall we say 'classic' – tale of the wee man trying to buy 250,000 bricks at B&Q. Says Andy: "'Oh,' says the lassie, 'are you building an extension?' 'Naw,' says he, 'ah'm buildin' a BBQ.' 'You don't need 250,000 bricks to build a BBQ,' she says. 'Ye dae if ye live oan the 34th flerr.'"

14

Keeping It in the Family

Families are the bedrock of our way of life, but they also provide us with some of our funniest moments.

GLASGOW Airport is attempting to reunite owners with their lost teddy bears that have accumulated at the airport. A Glasgow reader tells us that years ago a neighbour gave his young daughter an enormous pink teddy bear for her birthday, but he was not keen on it as it was stuffed with polystyrene spheres that he felt could be a choking hazard.

His solution was to quietly slip it into the bin, hoping the neighbour would not ask about it. His guile, alas, was undone the following week when the bin lorry roared into the street with said pink bear tied to the front grille.

MUCH debate amongst TV watchers about a daughter in her twenties going on *The X Factor* singing with her mother in a duet. As a young Glasgow woman of a similar age commented: "Imagine going on *X Factor* with your ma. I cannae go to the shop with my ma without wanting to put her in a headlock."

BRINGING up teenagers, continued. We hear of a Cambuslang teenager, finally forced into tidying his bedroom, who found so many of his clothes needing washed that he filled six bin bags with them. Not wishing to show his mother the amount, and not knowing how the washing machine worked, he secretly phoned his gran, who said that of course she would wash them. Not wanting his mum to find the bags, he put them outside the front door so that he could later drive over to his gran's with them. And then a charity collecting clothing donations gratefully picked them up.

MOTHERS of first babies can often be overly careful with their young charges. We notice a young mum confessing on social media: "I'll forever wish I'd double checked the worrisome red mark on my baby son's head before rushing him into the doctor's. The doctor rubbed it off. It was ketchup."

AND a reader in Partickhill found himself saying to his seven-year-old son, who asked if he could help decorate the Christmas tree: "Of course you can. First we string the lights on it, then we call Mummy through, who tells us how we did it wrong."

THE perils of new technology. A Hyndland reader tells us she shouted through to her husband in the kitchen to put the nuts she had bought in a ramekin and bring them through.

He was taking his time so she walked into the kitchen, where he was standing in the middle of the floor peering at his mobile phone where he had googled "ramekin".

SOME truth here, as Kieran Gormley comments: "Ryanair announce flight sales more often than my mam announces she's the only one who does anything around the house."

AND today's piece of daftness comes from a reader who simply emails: "I'm sure wherever my dad is, he's looking down on me. He's not dead, just very condescending."

HAVE you ever seen one of those little round robot vacuum cleaners that you leave to wander by itself around a room? Kenneth Gosnold tells us about his: "My dog doesn't like the robot vacuum and proceeds to bark at it. Today though the robot vacuum presented the dog with an empty Coke bottle it found under the coffee table. The dog and the robot vacuum are now best friends, with the dog dutifully following it around the house hoping it finds more treats for him."

EDINBURGH Zoo announced that their famous penguin Sir Nils Olav was 16 years old yesterday. It reminds a reader of the classic yarn of the chap who found a penguin wandering the streets of Edinburgh, and when he asked a passing police-man what he should do with it was told he should take it to Edinburgh Zoo. The next day the police officer spotted him still with the penguin and asked: "I thought you were taking it to the zoo?"

"I did," he replied. "And today I thought we'd go to the beach at Portobello."

TODAY'S piece of daftness comes from a Glasgow reader, who phones to tell us: "I built a model of Mount Everest to pass the time. A friend asked me if it was to scale. I told him no, it was just to look at."

A READER on the Neilston train into Glasgow heard young lads discussing the Facebook controversy about the company selling personal details. "I knew there was something dodgy about Facebook – that's why I deleted my account five years ago," one of them said triumphantly. "Naw it wusnae," said one of his mates. "It was because you took the huff at only getting three friend requests."

A READER heard a young chap in his local pub tell his pals: "I pulled up the duvet cover on my bed and my hand slipped and I accidentally punched myself in the face. Not to worry though – I've had it coming for some time."

CAT owners will identify with Glasgow comedian and *Strictly Come Dancing* performer Susan Calman, who passed on a conversation she had: "TV Producer: 'Do you have any photos of your cats?' Me: 'I'm sure I have a couple somewhere. I mean I'm not obsessed or anything.' TV Producer: 'Can you email them to me?' Me: 'Sure. I'll try to find some. Might take a while.' Immediately uploads 7,456 photos. Breaks internet."

TODAY'S piece of whimsy comes from a reader who emails: "If dogs could text you, they would fill your phone up with constant messages: 'When you coming home?' 'Where are you?' 'Are you nearly home?' If cats could text you, they wouldn't."

A READER sends us a message left on social media by sales manager Joe: "A mate overslept and had to get on a flight within an hour, so he shoved all the clothes on his bed into his suitcase. When he got to the airport he found out he'd packed his cat."

TOM Phillips reads that the most popular names for male dogs are Alfie, Charlie, Max, Oscar and Buddy and that the most popular names for female cats are Poppy, Bella, Molly, Daisy and Lola. Opines Tom: "It reads like the seating plan for a posh wedding."

A BEARSDEN reader confesses to us: "I was in the pet shop and spent quite a while reading the contents of their dog food before deciding on which one would be the most nutritional for our new puppy. I then drove off and took the kids to a McDonald's drive-through."

MARRIED life can be tricky. A Glasgow reader heard a chap in his local pub explain to his pals: "The dog ran in from the garden with its mucky paws, leaving a trail over the living-room carpet. 'Do something!' shouted the wife. Apparently reaching for my mobile phone to take a film of it wasn't what she had in mind."

TODAY'S piece of daftness comes from Foz, who declares: "Such a weird day – found a hat full of money in the street. Was also chased by a bloke with a guitar."

THE good weather has also seen folk besieging garden centres. One reader tells us: "No matter how hard I try looking after plants, feeding them, watering them, I can hardly get anything to grow. Yet a couple of old potatoes discarded in a corner of a garage have bloomed."

AND for sheer daftness, a reader in Knightswood emails: "I scared the postman today by going to the door naked. I'm not sure what scared him more, my naked body or the fact that I knew where he lived."

AN AYRSHIRE reader passes on an argument from a chap in his golf clubhouse who declared: "Women claim that childbirth is more painful than being kicked in the goolies, but I don't think that's right. I mean, have you ever heard a man a year after receiving such a kick saying he wouldn't mind you doing it again?"

OUR soldiers' tales can't stop the irrepressible Andy Cameron from claiming: "My late grandfather was the piper in the Black Watch and was first out of the trenches when an attack was launched.

"On his first day he was blowing away on his pipes when the bombs, bullets and mortars came flying overhead, prompting a comrade to demand, 'Andra', can you no' play something the Germans like?'"

OH dear, a colleague is eager to speak to me. Eventually I'm forced to look up and he declares: "Dad always said, 'Never do something that you'll regret later in life.' It was superb advice so I got it tattooed on the back of my neck."

AND a Bearsden reader muses: "I went round to visit my father who has retired and he showed me his new mobile phone, which he has in a protective case which looks strong enough to survive being run over.

"But all I could think about was us growing up as children when Dad was driving the family car and he didn't even bother to tell us to put on seat belts."

EVER buy a book online and a few days later the company asks you to review it? Thriller writer Simon Kernick commented at the weekend: "Just received a mental one-star review. It stated, 'I don't recall buying or reading this one. The cover doesn't ring any bells.'"

A GLASGOW reader swears to us that a chap in his local at the weekend was telling his pals: "My sister lost her cat last week." Says our reader: "One of his pals piped up, 'Did she put a piece about it on Facebook?' But the chap replied, 'I hardly think her cat's on Facebook.'"

A LANARKSHIRE reader tells us he was at the golden wedding celebrations of an old friend in a local hotel when the couple's son stood up and made an emotional speech about how much his parents meant to him and ended it with: "Thank you for having such a lovely marriage."

The man's father piped up: "And thank you for making it necessary."

A READER hears a woman in the West End tell her pal: "I can't believe, nearly 40 and I've suddenly got a big spot on my chin. Still, at least I can tell folk I have the body of an 18-year-old."

MOST dog owners can identify with Josh, who explains: "A character on TV opened a bag of crisps and my dog came running into the living room thinking it was me, so now she's playing with a ball she found and is acting like that's what she wanted all along."

TODAY'S whimsical observation comes from Ian Power, who says: "My girlfriend's started cooking vegetarian food because she says we'll have healthier and longer lives. I'm fairly sure she's right, but I'm not sure whether it's a price worth paying."

FOLK are still talking about the good weather at the weekend, and one or two people announced they had seen the first wasps of the year. As Joe Heenan put it: "There was a wasp in the house. I'm not saying it was big but I tried to kill it with a magazine and it took it off me and said, 'I've already read this one'."

15

Keeping Fit

We are all under pressure to keep ourselves fit these days, and fortunately some people can still smile about it.

GOOD to see older folk spending some time in council swimming pools to keep up their fitness. Many of them meet up with pals and make a morning of it. A Glasgow reader heard one such old fella say to his fellow senior-citizen swimmers the memorable line this week: "I'll have to go out – my skin's beginning to look like a corduroy bunnet."

SIMON Caine, appearing at this year's Edinburgh Fringe, reveals: "My dad says to me, 'I'm going to Tesco's, do you need anything?' I tell him, 'Yeah. Can you wear my Fitbit? I'm pretty sure I'm not going to hit my 10,000 steps.'"

A GLASGOW reader swears he heard a woman tell her pal in a West End coffee shop: "My goal was to lose a stone by Christmas. Just two stone to go!"

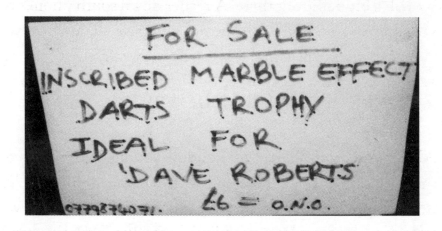

FOR SALE
INSCRIBED MARBLE EFFECT
DARTS TROPHY
IDEAL FOR
'DAVE ROBERTS
07798764071. £6 = O.N.O.

STILL good weather in Scotland, although it's not as hot and clammy as London apparently. As Robin Flavell described it: "You know it's hot when you're on the Tube and you're forced to wipe the sweat out of your eyes. And it's not even your own sweat."

HAVE you seen those folk on social media who go on about where they have run that day, even putting in a map? A reader heard a chap on the train into Glasgow tell his pal: "The best part about these punters posting their regular running routes is it makes it easier to avoid them."

IT has still been a bit chilly over the past few days. A Milngavie woman was heard telling her friends: "Who needs to spend all that money on Botox. I get the same result on my face just taking my dog out for a walk these mornings."

STILL a bit Baltic out there. A reader down south phones to say: "Have just worked out the one thing we all do when we have to walk in the snow – we can't stop ourselves looking at our neighbours' roofs to see how good their loft insulation is."

AND as Alistair Barrie in London commented: "One of the best things about travelling when it snows in the UK is watching horrified foreigners realise quite how badly we cope. You can see them thinking, 'Leave the EU? You can't even make it out of Tottenham Hale.'"

FOLK have been having difficult journeys out on the roads with all that snow. But sometimes we have to question their motives. As Scots writer Mark Millar revealed: "Just bumped into a pal who made a long, horrendous journey to school in snow while nursing flu. His reasoning? Didn't want to spend the day with the kids."

16
Ageing Beautifully

We have an ageing population, and *Herald* readers who are getting on a bit are happy to tell us about the dafter things that happen when you have had more birthdays than you care to remember.

A FIFE nurse swears to us that a patient recovering after an operation had to be told that he was going back into surgery as staff believed a swab had been left inside him and it had to be taken out. "Here's 10p," said the patient. "It cannae be worth more than that."

GROWING old, a thought. A reader in Edinburgh phones to tell us: "I'm at that stage in life where my bladder is at its weakest and my phobia of public toilets is at its strongest."

TALKING about ageing, a Pollokshields reader tells us: "The computer constantly tells me to protect my password. I find at my age all my passwords are protected by amnesia."

A GLASGOW reader was in his local pub where a fellow customer was telling his pals that he had gone for a check-up with a new doctor that he had registered with after moving.

The chap told his mates: "The doc said I should cut back on sugar in my diet, drink less alcohol and coffee, and reduce the stress in my life.

"So I said to him, 'Fair enough. But realistically what should I do?'"

GROWING old, continued. A Milngavie reader tells us: "My doctor was worried about me becoming a bit infirm and suggested I get a bar fitted in my shower cubicle. If he thinks a glass of wine will help, I'm all for it."

CONGRATULATIONS on Paisley Museum securing a £5 million lottery grant to help turn it into a world-class destination. Somehow the award provoked a Greenock reader to phone and tell us that Paisley folk are in fact known for their parsimony.

He said: "There was the story of the chap who was knocked down at Paisley Cross and a passer-by going over to see if he was all right. When the chap still lying on the road said he was only winded, the passer-by asked if he would like a fag. When he said he would, the chap asked, 'What pocket are they in?'"

GROWING old, continued. "When you realise the barber has cut more hair from your eyebrows that your head," says Jim Inglis.

WE asked for your GP stories, and Russell Smith in Kilbirnie recalls: "Many years ago as a young GP in Paisley I received a late call to an ailing old lady, three flights up in a tenement. After establishing that she felt 'chesty' and negotiating numerous layers of clothing I gave her a prescription to be told, 'That's no' me – she's across the landing.'"

And John Sim in Dumbarton says: "My old doctor in the

Gorbals was from the Middle East and was just getting to know some of his patients and their local phrases. He told of a phone call from a woman whose child was unwell, and when he asked what the symptoms were she said her son was 'spewing rings'.

"The puzzled doctor asked how many rings there were and could she bring some in for him to examine."

GROWING old, continued. A Lenzie reader tells us: "I'm at an age where I had an early night – and realised it was so early that I could still hear a neighbour mowing their lawn."

ONE of the big sellers over Christmas was the book *This is Going to Hurt* by Adam Kay, who describes his life as a junior doctor. He tells of a woman giving birth who had a cord prolapse and she had to rest on all fours while he wore a glove up to his shoulder so that he could insert his hand to keep the cord in place. Writes Adam: "The midwife led into the room the husband. 'Jesus Christ!' he says in a heavy Glasgow accent. The midwife remonstrated that she'd warned him I'd be holding the cord out of the way. 'You did,' he says, his eyes like dinner plates. 'You didn't say he'd be wearing her like Sooty though.'"

GROWING old, continued. A Troon reader writes: "Apparently I am now at that age where I 'look good for my age'."

AN AYRSHIRE reader tells us a chap in his golf club was relating: "Went to the doc's for my annual check-up. The practice nurse asked me to pop on the scales and, worried that I was going to get a lecture on putting on weight, I took off my boots, and then for good measure took my keys out of my pocket. 'Do you want me to wait while you shave your eyebrows?' she asked me."

GROWING old, continued. Says Mark: "When you reach 50, there's no point starting a film after 8 pm."

A SOUTHSIDE reader who returned from a shopping trip to Silverburn tells us: "I didn't know who to feel more sorry for – myself for not being able to remember where I parked my car, or the driver slowly following me through the car park hoping to get my space."

GROWING old, continued. Says David Donaldson: "I have discovered that you can recreate the wonder and excitement of childhood simply by ordering a series of small items on the internet. Then, four or five days later, packages arrive at your door and you have not the faintest idea what it can be or who sent them. It's a bit like Christmas in the fifties."

OUR growing-old stories included a reader who forgot to take his glasses off before going for a shower.

However Brian McAulay comments: "But you can't see when you take off your glasses. I thought my wife had got that exotic Euthymol toothpaste, only to find out when I got out the shower and got my specs on that I'd brushed my teeth with Germolene."

GROWING old, continued. A Kelvinside reader tells us: "The wife shouted through to ask if I had put some tennis on the telly. It seemed the noise I made bending down to pick up a dropped glasses case was similar to someone serving a tennis ball."

MORE on GPs as Alastair Stewart tells us: "An obituary in *The Herald* once told of a deceased doctor whose favourite story was when he looked out of his surgery window in the East End of Glasgow and saw one of his patients pushing a car. He decided to help the man, but when he tried to assist he was told, 'Beat it, doc – we're trying to steal it.'"

A REGULAR reader tells us her friends were discussing the effects of the menopause, with one woman explaining that she had bought special pants that have magnets inside them which somehow reduce your hot flushes. She added that she inadvertently bumped into a bowl of paper clips in her office when she was letting a fellow worker get past her, and the paper clips jumped out the bowl and attached themselves to the front of her skirt, much to everyone's surprise.

GROWING old, continued. Joyce Avery in Milngavie tells us: "My family were amused when I told them I had had laser treatment on my eyes to sharpen up my vision when reading the subtitles on the TV to help my hearing."

TALKING of singing, a Bothwell reader emails: "I hate it when I'm singing to an old song on the radio and the artist gets the lyrics wrong."

GROWING old, continued. Says Ian Noble: "I have been a keen race-goer for many years, and in the early days I used binoculars to watch the races, but with the introduction of big-screen televisions, I stopped using them. Now I'm back using them again – to see the big screen."

HAPPY birthday to the NHS. As an Edinburgh woman once declared: "I won't hear a bad word said about the NHS," adding: "That's because I have an NHS hearing aid." We are fortunate in Glasgow to have the state-of-the-art Queen Elizabeth University Hospital. Reader Lesley Wilson was having her appendix removed recently, and when her husband popped down to their local without her, a couple they knew asked him where Lesley was. "She's in the Queen Elizabeth," he replied. The wife of the couple said: "Wow! That's lovely. Where's she going?"

AN AYRSHIRE reader says a member at his golf club declared the other day: "Was at the doc's for a check-up and he asked me how much exercise I was getting. I asked him if sex counted, and he said yes. So I told him, 'None at all.'"

GROWING old, continued. A Knightswood reader tells us: "If I drop a 10p piece on the ground these days then it stays there. Bending down is a young man's game."

WE did end our false-teeth stories but Tony Martin in Vanuatu reminds us of a classic which deserves a repeat. Says Tony: "When cod angling in the Firth of Clyde was booming, a group of lads went out in a boat on a blustery day. One of the guys wasn't a particularly good sailor and was soon losing his breakfast, complete with his falsies, over the side. One of his mates had the clever wheeze of taking out his own falsies, hooking them into the mouth of a cod he had just caught and shouting that he had caught the fish that got his mate's teeth. His pal removes the falsies, and says, 'No, these are not mine,' and promptly threw them overboard. Hence two gumsy anglers coming off the boat that day."

TALKING of hospitals, a reader tells us he was recovering after an operation in one such establishment, and when a cheery nurse passed his bed and saw the piece of fruit a visitor had brought him, she chirped: "An apple a day keeps the doctor away." He couldn't stop himself from replying: "That's true! It's been three days since my op and I've not seen a doctor since."

GROWING old, continued. A Prestwick reader tells us: "I wear one of these wristbands that records how many steps I take during the day. I now wear it to bed at night as I get up to go to the loo that often that I might as well add it to my total."

A STUDENT doctor in Glasgow swears to us that he asked a patient, when taking his medical history, if there was anything that ran in the family that he should know about, and the auld fella replied: "Disappointment."

ROSEMARY Clark from Kilbarchan was in the accident and emergency department at Paisley's RAH when she overheard a fellow attendee being asked if he had taken anything for pain relief. "Yes," he replied. "A few cans of lager."

WE squeeze in a final GP story as Niall MacDonald tells us: "A doctor who practised on Paisley Road West had in his small consulting room a pair of footprints marked on the carpet. It must have confused some patients who thought it had something to do with some esoteric treatment. The truth was simpler – if he placed his feet in the marks he could swing his 5-iron without hitting anything.

"Must have been less pressured times in the NHS."

GROWING old, continued. A reader confesses: "I was telling a story involving a bus conductor. My son asked, 'What is a bus conductor?' When I explain, my daughter says she thought I had said 'a busking doctor'."

WE finished our GP stories, so let's call this a Millport story. Says reader Margaret McGregor: "My late father was very friendly with the Millport GP, who told him that he was called out to see a young boy who became unwell on coming home from school. Examining the boy, the GP asked if he passed water that day. The boy replied no, he hadn't, as he had come home by the back road."

GROWING old, continued. Says a Muirend reader: "Not sure if it's an age thing but I found myself visiting neighbours who had a child gate installed at the bottom of the stairs. I needed to go upstairs to use the loo but couldn't work out how to open the child gate. Gave up and waited for someone else to go upstairs."

MORE on older folk and technology, as Shauna Wright declares: "I'd like to thank whoever told my mum that WTF means 'wow that's fantastic'. Her texts are so much more fun now."

WE pass on the observations of *Still Game* actor Sanjeev Kohli, who muses: "Feel sorry for this generation who have never used a phone box. It's not the same, urinating into a mobile."

A PICTURE of the warning sign about not putting bags of popcorn below the automatic hand dryer in a cinema toilet reminds Celia Dearing: "I was in the Ladies at the old Dumfries and Galloway Hospital, and as there was no shelf I rested my handbag in a sink. The motion-activated tap came on, pouring water into my bag. Mod cons, huh!"

A NEWS story stated that using mobile phones after 10 pm can trigger depression and loneliness, according to research.

A reader tells us: "I used to take my mobile phone to bed but stopped after I dropped it one night and thought it had bounced under the bed.

"I got down on my knees, peered under the bed and couldn't see it.

"Without thinking, I noticed my phone lying beside my leg so I picked it up and used the light in the phone to look for it under the bed. Then the penny dropped."

TODAY'S piece of daftness comes from an Ayr reader who emails: "I found out I was colour-blind yesterday. To be honest, it came totally out of the green."

17

No Longer with Us

Readers recall the lighter moments of those who have passed away in the last year.

THERE is genuine sadness at the death of former Thistle manager John Lambie, with ex-players emphasising he was a superb tactician, which was often overlooked as people concentrated on his colourful sayings. We at The Diary were among those promoting John's comments, such as after one particular bad game: "I'm away home to put my head in my birthday cake – the cake's in the oven." But not all his cheeky remarks were about football. Former player Derek Whyte said: "When John picked up a lifetime achievement award he was asked what his greatest moment was. We, of course, expected him to say something about his work with Thistle but instead he answered, 'The first time I took Viagra.'"

MIXED views on Hugh Hefner, founder of the *Playboy* magazine who died at the age of 91 last week. One reader does make the interesting point, though: "It shows you how long Hugh Hefner lived that his first wife's name is Mildred, and his last wife's name is Crystal."

THE sad death of New York chef Anthony Bourdain reminds us of when he was filming in Glasgow and went to a martial-arts session in the city and was paired up with a smaller Glaswegian. Thinking it would be an easy match, Anthony later confessed: "It was like running into a fire hydrant. He crushed my ribcage like a box of biscuits. I ended up pounded into the mat again and again by the murderous (yet relentlessly cheerful) garden gnome."

THE death of nightclub owner Peter Stringfellow was announced yesterday, and writer and presenter David Baddiel recalled: "I met Peter Stringfellow once. He had a sense of humour beyond the haircut. I asked him what he'd be doing if he hadn't ended up running strip clubs. He said, 'Two words: benefit fraud.'"

THE Herald obituary on showbiz writer Gordon Irving, at the grand age of 99, reminds us of the neatly typed letters Gordon used to send the Diary from his home in the West End's Kelvin Court, courteously telling us a neat yarn about an old music-hall act who had been in the news. Gordon was also a collector of classic jokes and once told of the young reporter from Glasgow who was flown out by his newspaper to cover the after-effects of a particularly violent earthquake in southern Europe. Getting a bit full of himself he filed a graphic story that opened with the colourful prose: "God sat on a mountaintop here today and looked down on a scene of ..." The reporter got a cable back from his editor in Glasgow declaring: "Forget earthquake. Interview God."

SAD to hear of the death of Glasgow-born former Speaker at Parliament Lord Martin who never hid his working-class roots. I remember when he was chairing a prestigious debate at Glasgow University and an SNP speaker joked that his party held a raffle in Possil where the first prize was an alibi for a fortnight. This stirred the then Michael Martin who declared: "My wife, Mary, comes from Possilpark. She'll want a word with you."

THE death of Barbara Bush, the former First Lady in America, was covered in our sister paper *USA Today*, which recalled one incident: "Mrs Bush described Geraldine Ferraro, her husband's opponent for vice president in 1984, 'I can't say it, but it rhymes with rich.' She later apologised and said she had the word 'witch' in mind."

WE mentioned the sad death of former Thistle manager John Lambie, and Paul Drury, working in public relations, tells us: "I once had the daunting task of persuading John to dress up as a samurai warrior to promote a car sponsorship deal with Thistle. John was up for it, particularly when he was trying on the various pieces of his Japanese suit for the photo shoot at the ground. 'What's this, son?' he asked as he got changed in his manager's office. He was holding up a confusing piece of warrior kit. 'It's a kind of apron,' I said. 'Ah,' said the Whitburn man, 'I know how to put wan o' them on.'"

MUSIC fans are saddened by the death of veteran music writer and former *New Musical Express* editor Roy Carr who, in a roundabout way, owed his writing career to holidaying Glaswegians. Roy told the story he was in the band supporting the Rolling Stones at Blackpool's Winter Gardens during the Glasgow Fair in 1964. One of the Stones kicked a Glasgow chap trying to get on the stage, a riot ensued, a piano was trashed and Blackpool Council banned the Stones. Roy phoned the *Daily Express* to tip them off, and the fee they paid him was more than he earned from playing that night, so he decided to become a journalist.

WE also note the sad death of Alex Dickson, the former programme boss at Radio Clyde who never failed to contact the Diary if he felt we had maligned Radio Clyde, which in truth happened regularly. Anyway, Alex was probably at his most relaxed when he was interviewing authors for his book-review programme. He once recalled being taken to one of London's most expensive restaurants with Scots writer Alistair MacLean. Alistair took one look at the metre-wide menu, written only in French, and amid the hushed tones of the restaurant told the waiter, "I'll just hae a wee bit o' fish and chips." And fellow thriller-writer Frederick Forsyth took Alex for a drink then realised he had forgotten his wallet, and borrowed cash from Alex. Three times Forsyth tried to pay him back but Alex refused, telling him he preferred going round telling folk Frederick Forsyth owed him money.

FOLK are still recalling the humour of the late Ken Dodd, and Tom Peck says: "Ken was on the Michael Parkinson show where he explained, 'If you tell a joke in Glasgow, they laugh. In Birmingham, they don't.' When Parky asked, 'Why's that?' he replied, 'They can't hear it.'"

JUST as an aside to the death of funnyman Ken Dodd, we are reminded of our former editor Harry Reid's book *Deadline*, in which he chronicles the ups and downs of the Scottish press, and in which he tells of former *Scotsman* editor John McGurk, when he was a young reporter, making conversation with a local minister. John had told Harry: "I went to this minister, and I was trying to get a story, and on his sideboard there's a picture of Ken Dodd, who was a pretty popular comedian at the time.

"To try and break the ice, I say, 'Ken Dodd, is that someone you know?' And he looked at me and looked at the picture, looked back at me and said, 'That's a photograph of my wife.'"

OUR mention of the late evangelist Billy Graham's rallies in Glasgow remind John Gilligan: "My uncle Willie attended the one held at Ibrox. He used to tell me that the pastor invited people to come forward and be saved. A wee Glesga fella raced on to the park and the pastor asked if he had come to be saved. 'Naw, Reverend, it's jist that ah've always wanted to walk on that pitch!' he replied."

OH dear, just back from a holiday and immediately a colleague tracked me down. He cornered me to tell me his words of wisdom: "Just a tip for mourners. Cheer yourself up the next time you go to a funeral by simply hiding a £20 note in the back pocket of your black suit."

SOME newspaper corrections require a wider audience. Ewan MacColl was a famous folk singer who, although born in England, was very proud of his Scottish parentage.

He married Peggy Seeger, and the *Guardian* newspaper has printed the correction: "A review of Peggy Seeger's memoir quotes her description of her early impressions of Ewan MacColl and how they fell in love, saying he had a 'hairy, fat, naked belly poking out and was clad in ill-fitting trousers, suspenders, no shirt, a ragged jacket and a filthy lid of a stovepipe hat aslant like a garbage can'. The context we omitted was that MacColl was appearing in a production of *The Threepenny Opera*."

SAD to hear of the death of former Glasgow Tory MP Teddy Taylor, who was an extremely charming man despite his right-wing views – it must have been his time as a *Herald* journalist. Teddy was wise enough in Thatcher's day not to actually put the word Conservative on his election leaflets, and when asked why his Cathcart leaflet was printed in red, he merely replied he felt the colour stood out. Folk who voted for him thinking he was Labour, well that was just an unfortunate error.

OUR mention of the late Harry Dean Stanton being in Glasgow to film Bertrand Tavernier's sci-fi classic *Death Watch* reminds a colleague of Tavernier saying in an interview years later that there was an Orange parade going past their hotel when they were in the city. Harry, he said, found it so astonishing he immediately phoned his friend, film star Jack Nicholson. Said Bertrand: "I could hear Nicholson on the other end of the line, only half awake, and trying to understand what was happening. Stanton made him listen to the Protestant parade. What a wonderful moment."

THE late Bruce Forsyth was of course a keen golfer, and in the seventies he took part in a pro/celebrity golf match at Gleneagles which included Sean Connery, Bing Crosby and Burt Lancaster. Bruce later recalled in his biography that there was a reception and dinner afterwards in the hotel, and the following morning the hall porter found actor George C. Scott asleep in a chair, still wearing his dinner suit.

When the porter gently woke him and asked if he could get him anything, George C. replied: "Get me a cab. I'm going home."

"What about your clubs, Mr Scott?" continued the porter.

"Burn 'em," said the actor.

SAD to hear of the death of former footballer Ray Wilkins, one of the English stars brought north to play for Rangers in the late eighties. Years later, in 1996, he was asked by a

Herald sports journalist if he had any tips for Hearts, who were facing Rangers in the Scottish Cup final. "They could board up the goal," was his cheeky reply. Turned out he wasn't off the mark. Hearts went on to lose 5–1.

JOURNALISM lost one of its singular talents with the death of Albert Morris at 91, who in his day wrote erudite but always amusing columns in *The Scotsman*. He once was guest speaker at a dinner, and, as he recalled afterwards: "I had to hire an evening suit as mine was being cleaned to rid it of collected waiter droppings. It had what seemed a handkerchief with a smartly serrated edge showing at the top pocket.

"During my speech, I reached for the supposed handkerchief, which resisted my increasingly desperate tugs. Suddenly, there was a rending sound and the article – a wretched sliver of cloth attached to a cardboard base – was revealed in all its tawdry tastelessness. My astonished face, doubtless resembling a ripe nectarine, set the tables in a roar and my gas at a peep."

SAD to hear of the death of former Morton chairman Douglas Rae, who kept the club going for decades. His old chum Arthur Montford was also a director of the club, and Douglas once told us of going by train with Arthur to a game in Berwick and asking the young lad pushing the refreshment trolley for a sandwich. The chap said he had only one left, and couldn't give them it as it was past its sell-by date. When they asked how far past the date it was, he replied, "Ten minutes."

It turned out that the sandwiches he carried were only stocked for four hours, and as it was four hours and 10 minutes since he brought them on board he couldn't sell it – no matter how much they protested. "Things can only get better," said a hungry chairman. They didn't. Morton lost 2–0. "We'll bring our own piece next time," Douglas muttered to Arthur afterwards.

COMEDY fans noted this week that writer and performer Spike Milligan would have been 100 yesterday if he had lived this long. Steve Doherty still has the letter he got back from Spike years ago when Steve wrote to him when he was a teenager asking Spike how he could become rich and famous. The typed letter simply states: "Dear Stephen, Rob a bank. Regards, Spike."

18

A Sporting Chance

Scotland is a sporting nation – although mostly from watching sport rather than participating in it. Here are our readers' tales from the sporting grounds.

THE Portugal–Iran World Cup game got a bit tousy towards the end, with players constantly haranguing the referee. Ed Hunter tells us: "It's not a new thing. Brian McGinley, the ex ref, tells the story of Aberdeen leading by a goal against Rangers with 89 minutes played. They are trying to keep the ball by the corner flag to waste time when Ian Ferguson takes the hump and puts in a life-threatening tackle. Pandemonium! McGinley and his linesman are trying to break up the ensuing melee and avoid widespread red cards. He decides to blow for time-up and get everyone up the tunnel. As he runs off the park Rangers manager Jock Wallace points at his watch and yells, 'It isnae full time, McGinley! Whit's yir rush?'

"'I'm going to a wedding,' responds Brian.

"'Is it yir mither an' faither?' says Jock."

ENGLAND, of course, beat footballing minnows Panama, and reader James Thomson in Jordanhill tells us: "It reminded me of overhearing a man on Buchanan Street on his phone the day the World Cup group draw happened. Clearly he had just heard England's group. All I heard was, 'Panama? Flipping Panama! Who else did they get? Suez and the Crinan?'"

DON'T know what to make of the stories claiming champion cyclist Bradley Wiggins took prescription drugs to enhance his performance. A West End reader comes to his aid and tells us: "I've got nothing but respect for Bradley. I once took drugs and tried to cycle and ended up swerving to miss a dog and ended up in the canal."

ONE or two folk unhappy with the road closures for the European Cycling Championships in Glasgow but most liked seeing the city portrayed across Europe. We liked the musings of actor Gavin Mitchell, who opined: "Amazed that nobody's dug has run oot in front of them, no half bricks have bounced off their spokes and nobody has stopped them and asked them for a light!" And a local cyclist watching the time-trial competitors head back in past Springburn: "Ach, I've gone faster myself on this stretch. Mind you, I was being chased by a bunch of neds at the time."

GREAT win for Scotland against England at cricket this week – hard to beat a relaxing day in the sun, having a beer and watching the game. Anyway a reader in London was in his local when the result came on the telly and a chap further up the bar opined: "I knew they sold a lot of cricket bats in Scotland – I just didn't realise they used them for playing cricket."

OLD joke time – "You've got yourself a keeper there," said the chap in the pub, looking at a picture of his mate's new girl-friend. "So you think she's good-looking?" said his delighted pal. "Naw," replied his mate. "She looks like Alan Rough." We only mention it as we would like to congratulate former Scot-land keeper Roughie becoming a director of Partick Thistle. A colleague once told us he was at a Sportsman's Dinner when the chairman introduced guest speaker Roughie by saying Alan's old goalkeeping gloves were to be used in the fight against worldwide infection. "After all," he said, "if you wear these, there is absolutely no chance of catching anything."

OUR mention of the great footballer Jim Baxter reminded Paul O'Sullivan: "In the late sixties Baxter was called for an interview with Leeds United, the most successful club in England at the time. Manager Don Revie, trying to put pressure on Baxter, said, 'I've been asking around about you. It seems that football comes a long way behind birds, booze and fast cars in your list of priorities.'

"'You're remarkably well informed,' replied Slim Jim."

GOOD to see Scottish fitba' is back after we tried to get used to all those silky skills at the World Cup. As junior football side Easthouses Lily Miners Welfare, who play in the East of Scotland League, explained on social media at the weekend: "Our friendly today was abandoned at 3–3. An opposing player attempted to choke-slam the referee before the referee gave him a clothesline and it ended all square."

And no, a clothesline was not the ref helping him hang out his washing.

NOT everyone is into the World Cup, though. David Steel tells us: "A bit bored of the World Cup so a friend said on social media he was going to watch *Gregory's Girl*. A friend then posted that in 1990 he had a German girlfriend who got a teaching placement at Abronhill High School, the setting for the film, in Cumbernauld. He said he went with her to show her where it was. As they arrived in Cumbernauld she burst out crying. Thinking she was nervous about her placement he pulled over and said, 'Don't worry, the kids will love you.'

"'It's not that' she replied, 'I'm so ashamed of what my country did here.'

"He comforted her with, 'Naw, we did this to ourselves – I'll take you to Clydebank tomorrow.'"

OUR mention of Rangers legend John Greig reminded Hugh Brennan of his days teaching in the old Irvine Royal Academy. Says Hugh: "George Maxwell, the Kilmarnock defender, was on the PE staff and there had been an incident in a Rangers–Killie match in which Sandy Jardine was sent off. George was left lying on the Ibrox turf injured when John Greig bent over him. 'I saw John leaning over you, was he concerned about your health?' he asked George. 'Aye,' he replied. 'He said, get up, ya b******, and I'll knock you back doon again. I thought it wiser just to stay where I was.'"

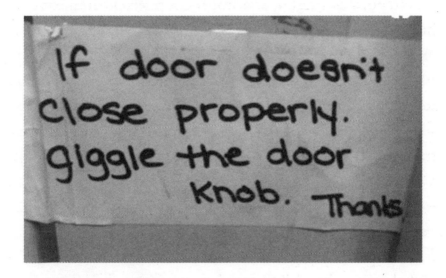

MOTHERWELL Football Club now has a Spanish and a French player, with Alex Rodriguez Gorrin joining Cédric Kipré. So the club had them attempting to understand Scottish Twitter messages which the bamboozled players tried to read out while being interviewed at the club's summer training camp in Ireland. Among the messages that had them stumped were: "Why dae folk ask babies stupid things like 'Ur getting awfy big, aren't ye?' As if the wee one's gonna be like, 'Aye, Moira, yer spot on, Ah'm on the protein.'" And the sublime: "I'd be so ragin' if I was a sniffer dog. A dug with a job. All your pals doon the park sniffing backsides 'n' you cannae cos you're on backshift."

THE fractious behaviour of some World Cup players has had readers reminiscing about Scottish footballers. Says Mike McGeachy: "I was at a function where Dunfermline stalwart Jim Leishman was a guest speaker, and he recounted the tale of a Pars game against Rangers at East End Park. Jim was given the unenviable task of man-marking Gers legend and captain John Greig by manager Harry Melrose. 'Gie him a kick whenever ye can, Jim,' said Melrose, 'and if ye can get him carried off, so much the better.' Jim said, 'Boss, but whit if I get sent aff?' Melrose replied, 'Dinna worry about that, son – they'll miss him mer than we'll miss you.'"

TALKING of Rangers, sad to hear of the death of Ibrox legend Jimmy Hubbard, who scored 65 of the 68 penalties he took for the club. Jimmy Brown, the ex-Kilmarnock keeper who had saved one of the three, was years later boasting about the feat at a coaching occasion. Hubbard bet him a pound that he would put 10 past him there and then. He later recalled that he hit the first four to the left and realised that Brown expected the next one to go right, so he hit the next six to the left also, with Brown always diving to the right. Incidentally Jimmy's son once wrote to *The Herald* about football-club discipline and said his dad cycled to Ibrox thinking it would be good for his fitness but was summoned to manager Bill Struth's office and told to get rid of the bike as it was "totally inappropriate" for a Rangers player.

WHEN the fitba' season is over fans' thoughts turn to other subjects. A Jordanhill reader tells us he was on a fans' forum where someone asked: "What do you do when the wife is out and you have the house to yourself?" One fan replied: "I put on my wife's clothes and go around the house criticising everything in the hope that I can finally find out what enjoyment she gets out of doing it."

THE appointment of Gerry Britton as Partick Thistle's new chief executive reminds us of when Gerry was dismissed as co-manager of Thistle some years ago and was surprised to be called into Springburn Jobcentre for an interview under its employment restart scheme. "We'll give you every assistance to get back into the world of work," an earnest-looking young woman stated. Pointing to the back page of the newspaper he'd brought with him, Gerry said he'd spotted just the opening, and asked if he could get an interview for the then-vacant Manchester City job. There was an awkward silence before Gerry explained he was joking.

CONGRATULATIONS to Auchinleck Talbot winning the Scottish Junior Cup at the weekend. It perhaps allows us to repeat that old Ayrshire joke of the chap from rival village Cumnock declaring Auchinleck "is only good for fitba' players and hoors". The large chap further down the bar angrily said his sister lived in Auchinleck. Altogether now: "What position does she play?" asked the Cumnock man.

WE are going to start with sports news, as it is reported that St Mirren manager Jack Ross is poised to become the new Sunderland manager. A fan of Sunderland rivals Newcastle emails us with the comment: "So Jack Ross has been appointed as the new Sunderland manager. A lot of people with a casual interest in football might be asking, 'Who?' The answer is, of course, that they are a small English club in League One."

MOVING story in *The Herald* about former Rangers star Willie Henderson planning to trek the Sahara for charity in memory of his daughter. It reminds us of when boxing great Muhammad Ali fought an exhibition bout in Paisley ice rink and was introduced to Willie. After seeing Willie's weather-worn visage, Ali asked him what he did for a living, and when Willie told him, Ali replied: "Football! I'm glad I stuck to boxing."

IT'S the 10th anniversary of the death of Celtic player and manager Tommy Burns, who is still remembered with affection by all who knew him. Former Rangers player Ally

McCoist recalled the other day that when they were both in the Scotland team, the squad was assembled in St Andrews for a "Show Racism the Red Card" photo opportunity.

Ally, as usual, was late, much to the rest of the players' chagrin.

"I go, 'Sorry, lads; sorry, lads.' They are all raging at me, raging. So I go to sit down but I don't have my card to hold up for the picture. Tommy leans over and goes, 'Haw, gie that Orange b****** that "Show Racism the Red Card" will you?' Brilliant! I mean what a line."

IT'S just over a month away, and a reader emails: "I stopped a bloke in the street and said, 'Can you help me? I'm looking for a rubbish tip.' He replied, 'England to win the World Cup.'"

SO Rangers caretaker manager Graeme Murty has stepped down after the board of the club announced they had "relieved him of his duties".

Sad day for Graeme, but words of support from BBC Scotland football commentator Jim Spence, who says: "Being relieved of your duties doesn't have to be a cause for shame.

"Mrs S relieved me of my edging duties in the gairden last night on spurious grounds of incompetence.

"I didn't feel any shame at all."

THE *Herald* reports that Rangers striker Kenny Miller is looking likely to have played his last game for the club after a fall-out with caretaker manager Graeme Murty. Kenny, of course, was once the subject of one of the most lyrical commentaries on the radio when he came on as a substitute in a game against Kilmarnock and scored the winning goal in a 3–2 encounter. The Radio Clyde commentator Dougie McDonald, clearly a fan of Procol Harum, had obviously been waiting for that moment as he declared over the airwaves: "Kenny Miller! Rangers are ahead! As the Miller tells his tale, Killie's face, at first just ghostly, turned a whiter shade of pale!"

WE asked for your amateur fitba' tales, and a reader in London tells us: "I worked with a colleague who told me about playing against a real nutter in his pub team league. After having the ball taken off him on several occasions the guy lost his rag and told my colleague, 'Do that again and I'm going to my car after the game and getting a gun.'

"'I've seen your shooting today,' my colleague replied, 'so I'll take my chances.'"

FORMER Celtic player Chris Sutton is making a name for himself as a controversial football commentator on the telly. He is accused, however, of always having a go at Rangers. A supporter of the Ibrox club contacted Chris on social media and asked: "Is there a football agenda you can talk about without dragging Rangers into it? You're obsessed."

Chris merely replied: "Champions League?"

TOO much snow even for the keenest of golfers. Over in Australia, though, Gordon Gosnold tells us about a friendly foursome which ended with one frustrated player taking three shots to get out of a greenside bunker. After raking the bunker, as you do, he picked up his bag of clubs and threw it into the lake beside the green before trudging towards the clubhouse.

Says Gordon: "Not sure how to proceed, the other three are pleased to see their comrade stop, turn round, and wade into the water and retrieve the bag, which he dragged to the side. He then unzipped the side pocket, retrieved his wallet and keys – and tossed the bag back in."

A GOLFER in Ayrshire was telling fellow members in the clubhouse that his five-year-old grandson asked him if he could caddy for him. Continued the golfer: "I told him that he had to be able to count, as he would have to keep my score, so I asked him what six and five were. He said nine, so I told him he's definitely got the job."

A SCOTTISH newspaper wondered if seagulls are the latest threat to Scottish football after one of them dropped the carcass of a dead pigeon in the goalmouth at the Queens Park match the other night. It follows on from claims that the raucous seagulls at Aberdeen are becoming louder and more belligerent. One person who might agree is Diary reader Bill Lothian, who once told us about his referee pal recounting that junior football fans at an Ayrshire ground began pelting the opposition goalkeeper with bread. The ref thought that was odd until minutes later when a squabble of seagulls swooped down for the bread, distracting the keeper as he tried to deal with a dangerous cross into his box.

BILL Lothian was playing in a seniors golf tournament at Dunbar which was a "shotgun foursomes" where 18 groups start off on different tees at the one time, signalled in the past by firing a shotgun that everyone could hear.

Says Bill: "Organisers said it would be launched by the sound of a horn, then explained in the pre-competition instructions, 'We have tried launching a rocket to let everybody know when to start in the past, but unfortunately this led to the Dunbar lifeboat being wrongly called out.'"

WE are trying to be magnanimous about England's results so far in the World Cup but the gushing triumphalism of the commentators is hard to take. So we pass on the observation of the late John Lennon's wife Yoko Ono, who declared on social media: "Who will win the World Cup? A child who believes in a peaceful world." We recommend you pass on her observation to the next England supporter.

AND Sarah Simmer observed: "If you think asking a Scottish person, 'How are Scotland doing in the World Cup?' will shake them in any way, you have fundamentally misunderstood the collective character of Scottish people, who have long ago transcended any hopes of 'victory' in any aspect of life. We're past that."

TALKING of golf courses, congratulations to Jane McDonald becoming the first female captain of Kilmacolm Golf Club.

We remember years ago when then Celtic chief executive Terry Cassidy won the Captain's Plate at Kilmacolm, and Rangers fan Andy Cameron, presenting the prizes, joked that it was the only silverware Cassidy would have seen for a while. Changed days, eh.

And was it not Kilmacolm Golf Club where so many ageing members had gone through hip and knee replacements that the joke was there was more titanium in the members than there was in their golf bags?